Summer Days Hot Nights

Memories of a '50s/'60s Teenager:
Sex, Cars, Golf, & Rock 'n Roll

Brian Doyle
with
John W Prince

HALLARD
PRESS

Cover Design by Hallard Press LLC/John W Prince
Cover Image: Adobe Stock
Page Design, Typography & Production by Hallard Press LLC/John W Prince

Published by Hallard Press LLC.
www.HallardPress.com   Info@HallardPress.com
Bulk copies of this book can be ordered by contacting Hallard Press LLC,
Info@HallardPress.com

Printed in the United States of America

Publisher's Cataloging-in-Publication data

Names: Doyle, Brian Watson, author. | Prince, John W., author.
Title: Summer days / hot nights : tales of a 50s/60s teenager : sex , beer , cars , & rock 'n roll / Brian Doyle with John W. Prince.
Description: The Villages, FL: Hallard Press, 2021.
Identifiers: LCCN: 2021910979 | ISBN: 978-1-951188-27-6 (paperback) | 978-1-951188-28-3 (ebook)
Subjects: LCSH Doyle, Brian Watson--Childhood and youth.. | Youth--United States--History--20th century. | Young adults--United States--History--20th century. | Norwalk (Conn.)--History--20th century--Biography. | United States--History--1945-1953. | United States--History--1953-1961. | BISAC BIOGRAPHY & AUTOBIOGRAPHY / Personal Memoirs | BIOGRAPHY & AUTOBIOGRAPHY / Cultural, Ethnic & Regional / General | BIOGRAPHY & AUTOBIOGRAPHY / Historical Classification: LCC E813 .D68 2021| DDC 973.921/092--dc23

Print ISBN: 978-1-951188-27-6
Ebook ISBN: 978-1-951188-28-3

Dedication

To
Raw Horsepower
&
Perfect Greens

FOREWORD

Growing up back in the 50s—well, it seemed a lot simpler then. Norwalk was a lot smaller than it is now. We had our neighborhood crew. Six or seven guys who hung out together and got in and out of trouble together. Not big trouble. Like one night we stole some watermelons from the back of a truck. The owner of the truck was also the owner of the watermelons. We ran; he chased, Brian tripped, fell down and split his knee, and needed stitches in the Emergency Room. That kind of foolishness; nothing serious. We were into cars and hot rods and chasing girls. We could tell what kind of car it was by the shape, even in the dark of night.

If you were under 16 there wasn't much you could do to make fast money except caddying at Shorehaven. Spend an afternoon lugging a golf bag in the blazing sun and get maybe three dollars and a buck-fifty tip. And we'd do it twice a day on weekends and holidays. On Mondays, when the course was closed to members, we all got to play. It became a way of life more than a game to some like Brian; he loved it.

During the summers there were beach parties practically

every day. After caddying we'd go over to the beach and the girls and boys would be there and we'd party right through and into the night. But again, it seemed simpler. We didn't have the drugs—certainly cigarettes and beer—but the real drug culture hadn't arrived in our city yet.

A lot of our time was spent playing jokes on each other and it seems pretty tame compared to today.

There were a lot of nick names back in the day and some stuck. Gino became Moose as he grew; Carman became Chico, he was Italian and quite a character. John Carpenter became "Jack" then "Carpie" as we got older Maybe that would seem out of place today, but it was harmless then.

I've lived in Norwalk my entire life. Married a Norwalk girl fifty years ago and we're still here. So are many of our friends.

Brian's book—this book—is like a trip back to the old days. I recommend it to anyone, from anywhere, who grew up in the 50s, and 60s. Its time travel you can hold in your hands. Most teenagers experienced many of the adventures, only they had different names. We will all remember, and smile, having had a great time in a great hometown.

GMV, Norwalk, CT
July 2021

Table of Contents

INTRODUCTION TO NORWALK, CT.

Oh Roger, Roger, Roger—if you could only see what they have done with your real estate purchase from Chief Mahakamo.

If you read one version of the history of Norwalk, you'll come away thinking that lawyer and master con man Roger Ludlow was the father, founder, patron saint, and arbiter of Norwalk. You'll see the venerable portrait in City Hall, "The Purchase of Norwalk from Mahakamo..." which was a Works Project Administration job daubed by some unknown, unemployed painter in the 1930s. The legend and myth have been enhanced for the modern age.

Not to say that Roger was a complete loser. He was the deputy governor of Connecticut in the 1640s. He wrote The Fundamental Orders of Connecticut, sometimes called "Ludlow's Code," with crimes listed in alphabetical order, and called one Mrs. Thomas Staples a "witch," was sued by the lady, lost, and retired to England where he was helped out by his buddy, Oliver Cromwell. He did found the city of Fairfield, adjacent to Norwalk, but his contribution to Norwalk is often overstated.

Norwalk was founded in two separate transactions in 1640 and 1641. And there is some confusion.

At the time the "civilized" world used two slightly different calendars: the Julian calendar which dated from the time of Julius Caesar, and the "new" Gregorian calendar dating from 1582.

It appears, according to some historians, that one Daniel Patrick purchased present-day South Norwalk, Rowayton, and West Norwalk on April 20, 1640. Ludlow purchased present-day East Norwalk and Saugatuck on February 26, 1641.

All according to the Gregorian calendar. You could discuss this well into the night over multiple beers and still not come up with a definitive answer as to who was first.

What we do know is that Mr. Patrick has been pretty well painted out of contemporary Norwalk history.

Mr. Ludlow's name is on the Founders Stone Monument in the East Norwalk Historical Cemetery (however he was actually buried in Ireland). His name is all over the place on street signs, shopping centers, a former school, and Ludlow Circle.

From the cairn atop the hill on the Silvermine Country Club you can see much of Norwalk and the white shores of Long Island in the distance. Then there's the annual Oyster Festival held to honor that old scene stealer, Roger Ludlow.

The post-World War II days made Norwalk a vibrant, next-door-to-New-York-City center. Veterans chasing the American Dream flooded the area, taking up the abundant jobs. There was a saying: "Norwalk could make anything you wanted," and that continued for years. Vacant lot today; subdivision tomorrow.

If you wanted to go anywhere back, then you probably had to go through Norwalk to get there. That all changed in 1958 with the completion of the Connecticut Turnpike. Norwalk became an "exit" and if you didn't have business there, you just kept on going.

A history, a continuity, a community that went back to the 1640s died on the asphalt and exit signs of the Pike.

Much like our teen years, it will never return.

Brian

The B&T Texaco purpose built '37 Ford coupe drag car. Photo probably taken at Dover Drag Strip in 1962. The car was later painted Easter green for the following three to four years. A Winner driven by a Winner.

CHAPTER ONE

Tales From the B&T Texaco

When I was 19 years old, I bought a gas station. That was in 1962.

It made sense because I was always a "car guy." 10W-30 ran in my veins. I had no knock on high grade. And I would have been hanging around cars and garages anyway. This way I could do what I wanted and make a living, at the same time.

It was also in the heyday of the gas station.

Gas was 26 cents a gallon. A pack of smokes went for 20 cents. A cold beer was even cheaper. And you could buy a good, used, three-year-old car for $200. And your dad was lucky to make $20,000 a year.

You couldn't pump your own gas back then. Not allowed. In fact, when you pulled into a gas station for a fill up a whole series of events usually took place. Your windshield was cleaned, someone dove under the hood and checked the radiator, oil and other fluids. Tire pressure was tested and adjusted. They might even check your headlights, tail and brake lights.

Compare that to today where you pay to pump your own gas, check your own fluids, pay a buck for 60 seconds of air and, if you go inside, maybe talk to a guy on the other side of a bullet-proof glass wall. Joyless! That's how I describe today's service station experience. Joyless and dehumanizing.

Anyway, it was 1962. I'd just graduated the year before from Norwalk High School with a freshly minted diploma certifying that I had attended just enough classes, turned in a sufficient number of assignments, learned to type proficiently, captained the golf team, and was never caught for serious trouble. So, they said "OK. Now you're on your own."

That was frightening for me.

Some people go through high school knowing exactly what they are going to do next. "I'm taking pre-med at State and then going to Princeton to become a brain surgeon. Or Harvard to become a lawyer. Or go to work in the family furniture store selling brightly patterned chesterfields. Or whatever."

There were some of us who really liked high school, even though we'd bitch and moan about it from time to time. Lots of free time, few responsibilities, caddy a bit for spending cash, a car, beer, smokes, girls, golf—what more could a guy ask for? Hell, I even had a couple of thousand dollars in the bank; savings from my caddying and doing odd jobs here and there.

How I got into the gas station business was completely accidental. A quirk of fate.

I was working at a Texaco station in New Canaan and was on my way home on a Friday night when I realized I was down to my last few cigarettes. I pulled into the General Store in the Broad River section of Norwalk, which shared the parking lot with the B&T Texaco.

Art Maestro, one of the General Store owners, noticed my Texaco shirt. "Hey, you wanna buy the B&T gas station?" He gestured across the parking lot. Art knew me from the neighborhood and, like a lot of smart adults in Norwalk, knew much more about the neighborhood people than he ever admitted.

I made some non-committal gesture that indicated, "I don't know. It's Friday night and I'm tired and, really, I just want to buy some smokes, have a beer, and get laid."

"No, no, not 'work' there," Art persisted. "Own it. You could own it." He was practically spelling out the words "o-w-n" to a complete cretin.

OK, I'll go along. "How much?" I asked peeling the cellophane off my smokes.

"A flat fee of $1,500 and it's yours," he replied nonchalantly as if he sold a gas station to a random teenager every day.

"So," I wondered aloud, "What happened to the last owner?"

Art gave me a long, sad tale of Old Bill who drank too much, let the tanks run dry, and opened only whenever his hangover demanded more medication. Somehow Art got involved and ended up with the ownership of the place. But he also had to run the General Store and didn't have time for a gas station.

I thought about it for about five seconds. "Yes. I'll have the money to you as soon as the banks open on Monday morning." Art brightened and smiled happily.

"Oh, one more thing, Art," I added. "Please get in touch with Bill and tell him to get his stuff out of there on Monday, because as of Tuesday, Brian Doyle will be doing business."

On Monday morning I paid Art his $1,500 and my father wrote up a bill of sale to cover my ass until I found out whether it was legal for a teenager to own a gas station in the State of Connecticut. My dad, with his excellent credit rating, helped open an account with Texaco and on Tuesday morning we were pumping gas.

Selling gas in 1962 was different than today. A motorist today might check the internet to find out where to buy the cheapest gas in town, drive there and fill up to save two cents a gallon.

Back then gas prices were less important and sales often depended on which direction the motorist was going. Going north on Route 123 the driver would pull into the B&T on their side of the street. Southbound drivers filled up at the Texaco across the street. No one knew why there were two Texaco's across the street from each other. I guess that no one wanted to make a left turn across traffic to fill up.

We had regulars—people who came every week or few days for gas or service. We got to know them and their cars and what they needed. They were like family, we knew their names, they knew us. We helped keep them on the road, and they helped us stay in business.

The first few of weeks were intense. Bob Crochetiere (aka "Crotchy") and I ran the place and worked long hours doing everything from filling radiators to counting the money to changing spark plugs. Business was more than good and soon John, my brother, joined us as a full-time mechanic. Between Crotchy and John they could fix anything that was driven, towed or pushed into the shop. My father became the bookkeeper. It was a family affair.

We did long days at the B&T—seven in the morning until nine at night, seven days a week. When we needed extra help part-time or on weekends we hired Paul Fusco (he gets his own chapter in this book) or some of the Depaulis boys, including Larry, who eventually bought the business five years or so later.

The B&T Hang-Out

Within a few months B&T was a full-service repair shop, gas station and, much to our amazement, a hangout for our friends, acquaintances, and some people we didn't even know.

It started small and quietly. Friends of ours started stopping by when they finished work to say "Hello," get gas, and have a cold beer from the General Store next door. (Maybe that was Art's strategy in the beginning: Sell the station to someone with lots of friends who would stop by every day and buy beer.)

Engineers, a lawyer, a judge, an artist, drag racers, hot rod drivers, mechanics, grocery store workers, a few nurses, and a core group of attractive young ladies who would stop by for a beer—but never a second helping of the extra spicy hot cherry pepper pizza. (Smart!)

They were a great group; always ready to help out: deliver a car, hold tools, adjust a light, get beer. Not having the benefit of cell phones back then, if you saw a bunch of people or cars at a place, the natural thing to do was stop and check it out. If you liked it you stayed, and came back again.

Most of the guys were late teens and early twenties, single and into the Yankees. The team was hot in those days and it seemed that Mickey or Roger hit a winning clear-the-bases home run every day. In the fall there was the World Series, football and plenty of baseball talk about the following season. Then there were the 'before the holidays' holidays and the 'after the holidays' holidays. It was a jumpin' place.

Of course, it had to happen. A few young ladies discovered that a bunch of young guys were having a fine time at the B&T hangout. So, they invited themselves in to join in the fun. Then their girlfriends joined them.

They may not have been able to figure out the attraction between the guys and the B&T, but hey, if the guys were there, the girls often followed.

Not that the guys minded. There was always plenty of ice cold beer (with more a few steps away) and our newest item: Uncle Joe's specialty pizza with extra virgin olive oil and cheese, hot sausage, onion and, to top it off, hot cherry peppers. You had to be both dumb and dumber to go back for seconds. Some did and paid the price within a few hours. But guess what? In a few days the walking wounded were back for more punishment. It was some kind of an addiction perhaps.

We even became a kind of dating service. Once we let the regulars know that so-and-so was going to be in town over the weekend, more people paid a visit—especially if Rope was coming back from his Navy base in Rhode Island about 125 miles away. That was always a good excuse for a party.

Part-time Hotel & Stable

I never would have predicted the next step: The B&T became a part-time temporary transient hotel/motel. Some of the guys, like Rope, who had joined up and were stationed nearby, would come home on weekends. But military pay was meagre, especially if you were a low end enlisted; they couldn't afford a motel. The only other choice was to stay with your parents.

That could be awkward when, as with Rope, the enlisted man was accompanied by a young lady to whom he was not legally and permanently attached.

A warm gas station with your car halfway up on the lift was super fine and kind of exciting. Hey, you knew you were safe. The doors were locked from the inside and you had a bathroom, heat, beer, and a radio. Life was good.

Naturally, that wasn't the end of it. No sir!

One warm fall night I was driving home after hours and saw a light on in the station. "Well," I thought, "that's not good." We kept the day's take in a hidden location until we could get it to the bank in the morning. Any robber stupid enough to go looking for it would be in for a nasty surprise. And no one had booked a "hotel room" that I was aware of.

I did a U-turn and went back, rolling into the parking lot and right up to the windows of the big shop doors. In the car headlights I can see something tied to the lift.

It was a horse.

We didn't repair, service, or fuel horses, so obviously there were some unanswered questions here.

Very quietly I unlocked and opened the main station door, which spooked the horse a bit. I moved silently into the shop and listened. From the back room I could hear the unmistakable moans of love conquering all.

It was all very perplexing. Someone (or two) had ridden into the repair shop in my gas station, on a horse, and were now apparently engaged in loud sexual congress.

Hey, Rope? Is that you?" I yelled out thinking that Rope had a night off or had joined the US Cavalry.

"No, Doyle. It's me," said a male voice from the back room.

"Who the hell is 'me?'" I demanded.

"Sorry about that. It's Johnny, here with my girlfriend." Johnny was one of our new hires. "We'll lock up and clean up any mess in a while." Pause. "Can we stay a little longer?"

"Of course, you can." Who was I to stop a nice young couple from getting a little loving in the back room of my gas station while stabling their horse in the service bay?

The following day, during the cocktail hour when everyone was present, I announced that, from this day forth: "There will be no more horses allowed inside the garage." Then I added, "You can ask Johnny why."

But the times were a changing,' as Bob Dylan noted, and the final cheerfulness, parties and overnights at the B&T seem, in retrospect, kind of desperate—as if we all knew that bad stuff was coming and we wanted to get in as much fun as possible before it landed.

That nasty-ass place called Vietnam, along with our nasty-ass politicians of the time, were destroying American lives, towns, and families at a high rate of speed.

Every one of us was afraid to open the mail for fear our number would come up. One by one our numbers did come up and our lives, at least the way we knew them, would never be the same.

For all kinds of reasons, I joined the Army before my number came up. (But that's another whole story that gets told later within these covers.) I sold the B&T to Larry Depaulis in 1968, and he owned the property for a number of years after that.

It was never the same again.

The War & Us. A Terrible Intrusion.

Many of the old B&T gang were 'in the war,' ripped away from their friends, family, girlfriends, cars, and the familiar anchors of their lives.

We all knew that we would smile and say 'Hello' and 'Goodbye' when we came home on leave, but Norwalk was never the same again.

The "war" was a new kind of thing for us. Our parents (at least no parents I knew) ever shared personal stories about their 'War years.' They never let down their guard;

never remembered or recounted their own personal horror show—except maybe in their nightmares.

So, we really didn't know what to expect. The only stories we got were about how they had to walk two miles to school, with no boots or gloves, in deep snow, year-round (uphill, both ways).

It was left up to our generation to admit to the sheer terribleness of what we saw and did, and the sheer awfulness of what happened to our friends.

I've seen grown, muscular, grizzled men ride up to the Vietnam Memorial on loud Harleys and trace out the names of their buddies and friends carved into the Wall, while silent tears run down into their unkempt grey beards.

Of course, they're heroes. They did what they were ordered to do, and they did it well. But their sacrifices didn't make any real, lasting, significant difference, at least in my opinion.

The educational authorities, in their infinite wisdom, don't teach "history" in the schools anymore. That would take time away from more important topics like gender studies or social media etiquette.

So, for the people like me, the denizens of the B&T's all over the country, I say "tell your stories." Just do it. Both you and the people listening may equally enjoy them, and they might even learn something useful. Like, not to repeat the same mistakes over and over and over.

That is one of the reasons why I decided to write down my tales.

A Car. A Job. A Little Bit of School.
Life was Good.

Norwalk was, at least among my friends and family, a city where cars were a vital part of life. Having a little grease under your fingernails was not a bad thing.

A new Ford in 1950 would cost less than $1,800. A few years later you could buy it second hand for $200. My brother, John, did. He went through a lot of cars. One of them was a '42 Mercury convertible he got for $50. In 1959 I bought a '55 Studebaker for $500.

Some of these cars needed a little work. But that was well within our skill set. Dropping in a new transmission or adding a new exhaust system was a weekend with a few buddies and a few beers. And these old cars were built to run forever.

Those of us who had cars also (by necessity) had jobs. From delivering newspapers to working in grocery stores to caddying at the Shorehaven Golf Club. There were no golf carts then—everything was a "carry."

We were entrepreneurs. At Christmas we'd decorate birch logs with plastic berries and leaves and sell them for $5 or $10 a pop. Shoveling snow, plowing driveways, mowing lawns, pumping gas. Working in a grocery store two or three days a week brought in $25 to $30. Caddies who hustled seven days a week and were liked by the pro could make over $100 a week during the summer season.

Lots of us had money in the bank.

This was also in the day when gas was 24 to 26 cents a gallon. So, you could go a long way on $40 or $50 a week.

Many of us also took motor shop at Norwalk High School. Mr. Guzman, our shop teacher, was a first-class mechanic, but couldn't keep order or students in the classroom. However, we would bring our cars into the shop, work on them with his help, improve the car, and get credits. You couldn't lose on that one.

Some of the guys were very talented and would drop a Caddy engine into an old Ford, install a strong transmission along with a few other goodies, and walk away from the competition during a race.

Most of us knew how to drive long before going to the DMV to take the test. In fact, a few of us had raced and also covered the measured quarter mile on the I-95 ramp near Swanky Franks in 15 seconds or less.

Some of the cars were classics, as were some of the young owners.

Like Dominic Peaburn's '58 Chevy Impala, black on black, lakes pipes which he would uncap for racing, with a continental tire kit on the back. It looked as long as a locomotive and sounded twice as mean and powerful.

The Super-Duper Ford

There are times when the unexpected and mysterious

occurred around the B&T, especially where cars and women are involved. Such was the case with Clay Wallace, the enigmatic older woman, and the Super-Duper Ford.

Clay was not a native of Norwalk; he came from Texas, although I never knew how or why he ended up in our fair city. Anyway, Clay had an accent: "He talks funny," most Norwalk people might say, referring to Clay's slow drawl and elongated words sprinkled with "Ma'am" and "Aw, shucks."

An older woman in Norwalk took a shine to Clay. Maybe she liked the way he talked. But I never got to meet her officially. She was always in the shadows or in the car when he stopped in at the B&T for gas or a yak.

Clay was a hotrodder and apparently the lady liked his accent so much that she bought him a new '61 Ford with 375 horsepower and a standard shift. We tinkered a bit with the engine and Terry "Kingston Trio" Kaestner of the "father & son" body shop welded on an exhaust bypass that produced some nice throaty music. I was the appointed driver for a while, and it regularly turned 13.7 at 102 mph.

Then, one snowy day we heard that Clay, the older lady, and the '61 Super-Duper Ford had moved on to parts unknown. Clay Wallace had left the building. We never heard from him again.

The Summer of Sheree LaRue

The Vietnam carnage had been underway for a bit and the young men who frequented the B&T social evenings were starting to dwindle at the call of Uncle Sam and the evenings needed spicing up.

As if on cue, late one spring evening a white 1966 Ford Mustang with a black interior and Mass. plates rolls in. No big deal until the driver got out.

A tall, leggy brunette with a seriously beautiful face and casually dressed in more money than we had seen in weeks eased herself out of the Pony and sashayed in.

"Is this the place to meet guys in their twenties?" she asked innocently.

There were only half a dozen speechless, twenty-something guys staring at her, their mouths hanging open, beer dribbling, and cigarettes dangling.

"Yes," someone finally said. "Yes, it is."

That was our introduction to Sheree LaRue, recently from Boston, wealthy, beautiful, experienced, willing to try anything (almost), and looking for excitement. She was, as we say in Norwalk, a "gamer."

During that spring and summer Sheree became a B&T regular—gas once a week and cocktails twice a week. We hung out, partied, drank, danced, made out, and stayed late. We teased her about her accent and her "cah" that she would "pak' in the B&T lot. The girls loved her, too, and she introduced 'foreign' wine to us.

She favored a Portuguese pink, *Mateus*, that came in an oddly-shaped green bottle and seemed much more classy that the any-Gallo-will-do brands that the local girls drank.

Of course, being beer drinkers, we didn't have a corkscrew. So, we pushed the cork into the bottle with a screwdriver. The girls, suddenly understanding class, informed us that the General Store next door had corkscrews and that we should invest in one. "I mean, what's the problem?" we asked. We had wiped the grease off the screwdriver with a rag.

Sheree was a storyteller and knew just when and how much fantasy to sprinkle in to keep the boys on the edge of their seats.

She was, she informed us, suffering from post-sexual withdrawal and needed some help real soon, or a trip back to Boston was in order. A few of the guys understood completely and she welcomed their advances.

So that we would be as educated on such matters as she was, she informed us that there is a BOOK and by now, she reckoned, most guys should have read it. "I mean I have only been in town for a couple of weeks and all the girls know of THE BOOK so I expect your pals should spend some time with it and adjust their approach."

Wow! Straight forward. No one blushed, so we figured it was okay.

Yeah, this was not your typical young lady. I say that because she told me and others that until she had studied THE BOOK, she had wasted yourself on about eight or ten guys before she was out of high school. She then laughed about a trick she gave it up to on the way home in a taxi. The driver was just taking her from a movie back to her dorm and Ms. LaRue needed a fix so she convinced him to pull over into the A&P parking lot. As she was taking off her panties and pulling up her school girl skirt, the cabbie nervously crashed his way into the parking lot.

Sheree LaRue was on the B&T most wanted list. She was accommodating and did her best to sample the single guys. Sheree told several of us that she even went up to the artist college and posed in the nude and that is where she met a lady in the raincoat who told her to pay a visit to the B&T. "You will be impressed with the guys because a few, if not all, have read THE BOOK."

No one was quite sure what she was doing, or did, in Norwalk. I believe that she kept that vague on purpose. At any rate, she was "transferred" or "promoted" and one evening announced that she was moving. Of course, we were all sorry to see her go. Some were perhaps more sorry than others.

We did hear later, through the always reliable grape vine, that she had settled in Bridgeport, where upon she succumbed to motherhood and bore twins. It's always good to know that a B&T alum had achieved success.

I always associate Sheree with the end of the party. The last hurrah. The spectacular summer ended, the Draft Board worked overtime, more friends and neighbors ended up face down the mud in Asian rice paddies, and America (and the B&T) would never again see a summer like the summer of Sheree LaRue.

CHAPTER TWO

Norwalk High School Confidential

"Boppin' at the high school hop" was how Jerry Lee Lewis described the era in 1958 in *High School Confidential*— the song and the movie. As I recall, the movie opened with The Killer kicking the crap out of his piano tied down on the back of a flatbed truck rolling through some small town and the local kids running after him. Girls screaming.

In the background of the movie there was sex (lots of it in our town), drugs (we didn't know so much about that), and rock 'n roll (which was the critical, essential, crazy, driving rhythm of our lives, especially the girls).

They (being the people who chronicle that time) usually forget cigarettes. Probably because they were ubiquitous. You could count the number of male nonsmokers over the age of 12 on one hand. Female on two hands. Lucille Ball sang the praises of Philip Morris and everyone knew what

LSMFT meant. *(Lucky Strike Means Fine Tobacco)*

You gave the Old Man a carton of cigarettes for Christmas. Of course! Cigarettes calmed, excited, gave people time to think, followed a good meal, went with a drink, made women glamorous, and were mandatory after sex. A smoke was what you had before, during, and after just about everything.

So here we were in 1959, hundreds of impressionable, unsuspecting 14- and 15-year-olds from a bunch of different area schools descending on Norwalk High School on the Tuesday after Labor Day to start the three years (that would, at times, seem like 20) and set the stage that would define our lives.

We called it "The Big House."

Some local wag said that, "All roads lead to Norwalk High School." After having gone to six different schools over nine grades, I know the author is correct.

Just the size of NHS was intimidating and the number of students who attended made it like a small city. From the late fifties into, say, the early sixties, over a thousand young men and women, hormones raging, arrived at the doors of NHS most mornings. (Once Brien McMahon High School opened in 1960, NHS was not quite as crowded.) Every other middle school in Norwalk leading up to The Big House had as many as 400 to 500 students, and there were many elementary schools.

The Norwalk Explosion!

Many of us who started school in and around 1946 to 1950, and lived south and west of the hospital, were affected almost daily by the tremendous growth of the city. You might start school at Jefferson. Then, a year later on, to Washington across the Boston Post Road. Next up was the newly completed Kendall school whose motto was "Knowledge is the Key to Life". Of course, that was only for a few years. Then it was off to West Avenue school for seventh grade. Next up was another new school for eighth grade, Ponus Ridge Junior High, totally in the opposite direction. Center Junior High for ninth grade, then on to The Big House on East Avenue.

The volume of surging hormones would fill a dozen Olympic size swimming pools. Think of that for just a moment when all Hell was breaking loose in the music world, movies, clothing, and many new words that these teenagers used and coined: *Cool Man, Groovy, Way Out, Daddy-o, Chicks, Das, Far Out*, and many more.

Many of the students had not seen some of their classmates from other schools for years. So, NHS became a giant melting pot. Considering what was being blasted through the air waves, TV, and Hollywood, it's no wonder there were a lot of wonderful, new, and different things to see, to sample, and to do. Most of us valiantly tried to complete the task, with varying degrees of success.

Guys like Dominick Peaburn.

He'd arrive at NHS in his brand new, black '58 Impala convertible and do a double loop around the block just so everyone could see and admire his magnificent car.

Dominick had a full-time job and he fit school in when his busy schedule allowed.

Dominick was also a resourceful entrepreneur. He would frequently sneak a case of beer into the boy's restroom. The beer was cold, of course, and he sold it for fifty cents a can. This was back in the day when a gallon of gas was like 23 cents a gallon. A six-pack back went for a buck—about 17 cents a can—so the profit margin was fantastic. It supplemented his income quite nicely, and (for some reason) he never got caught.

I think the guys bought and chugged their beers as part of their teenage rebellion. Smoking in the Boys Room was one thing; drinking beer took the rebellion thing to a whole new level. Smoking in the school building merited a two-week suspension; drinking beer would probably have resulted in a year on the street.

Sometimes I think the teachers overlooked this kind of shit because it was just a lot of extra aggravation to deal with it. And what harm did it really cause? Nobody got drunk on a can of beer. But it sure made you into one Hell of a rebel!

Auto Shop

Norwalk High School had several "streams" like the college stream, commercial stream, and shop.

Since so many students (especially the guys) had cars and drove them to school, it was only fitting to have a shop class dedicated auto mechanics. In addition to the goal of turning out competent mechanics for the local garages and manufacturing plants, the real appeal was that guys could upgrade and repair their cars for free—and get school credits for doing it. It was a win-win for everyone.

The auto mech teacher, Mr. Guzman was a nice, old guy who knew his cars. Unfortunately, he did not know much about teenage boys, beers, butts, and the willingness of teenagers to take multiple, long breaks—often.

So, it came as no surprise, once attendance was taken and Mr. Guzman opened the overhead door to let the guys bring in their cars, the great escape went into full-on mode. By halfway through the class many of the students had slipped away, and only half the class would be within the boundaries of the classroom. They might sneak in a test drive or just sit in their cars and listen to the radio: Elvis or some other popular singer.

Of course, Mr. Guzman soon noticed that more than a few of his students had disappeared, but he seemed uncertain about what to do.

After a few weeks, he worked out a plan where only

two to four guys were allowed to bring their cars to the shop, and then the door would be closed again. That kept quite a few around for the entire period, although there were a few who simply walked out when the door was open and never came back.

Word from some of the guys was that Mr. Guzman could be seen taking nips from his old Army canteen throughout the day. Maybe that's how he dealt with it.

Smokin' In The Boys' Room

In an era when everyone smoked, if you were caught smoking in or on the school property, the punishment was a two-week suspension. This was pretty harsh. A day, maybe; even a week. But a two-week suspension was a grade breaker. Plus, the school office sent a letter home to your parents, so now they were pissed, too.

So, there was an ongoing, unrelenting and constant war between the smokers who wanted a quick drag (usually in the boy's rest rooms) and the teachers who wanted to kick you out. I think it went on for so long that everyone actually forgot why they were having this perpetual battle. Guys smoked just to antagonize the staff; the staff tried to catch us just because they felt it was in their job description. It was like a crazy sport.

The longest period of the day was morning fourth. It was combined with school lunch (no break in between) and ran an hour and a half. For an avid smoker, that's a long time without nicotine. It was also a long time to go without having a break. During that time the smoke was so thick coming from the boy's room you did not have to go in for a butt. All you had to do was inhale while walking past.

One teacher, Mr. Guarancia, would barge into the boy's rest room every once in a while to see if he could catch a kid exhaling smoke, or with a lit butt between his fingers. When this happened one of the boys leaving would warn those inside that Mr. Guarancia was in view. He was so tall you could see his head bobbing above everyone else half a corridor away.

What unfolded this day requires that you follow each and every step intently.

The main characters in this little story are Mr. Guarancia and Willie Wyatt, an 11th grader. Willie was noted as having the most perfect, concrete-like duck's ass hair. It was piled up high and swept back around the sides of his head like dark, running water, to meet in exactly the back center. Very reminiscent of the north end of a south bound duck. I'm not sure what potion he used to keep it perfect, but it must have been slightly resinous and shiny.

Willie wasn't smoking as the scene opens, but he held an orange left over from his lunch. Old and dried up, the peel had dehydrated to a thin leathery texture that was not going to come off easily. Frustrated at the impasse with the peel, Willy wound up and let the orange go at the boys' room door expecting a big splat when it landed.

Did I mention that Willie was also a starting varsity pitcher for the NHS team and had a 86 mph fast ball?

The timing could not have been more perfect if they had practiced it for a thousand years.

Mr. Guarancia, no doubt expecting to collar a smoker, caught the orange directly in the middle of his tall forehead. THWACK! It was a noise like you expect to see in bright orange letters in a Marvel Fantastic Four comic. Thwack!

Then a sound we never expected to hear: A teacher swearing and cursing like a sailor, F-bombs exploding everywhere. We all stood entranced, motionless, cigarettes dropping from fingers, mouths open, smoke oozing out while we heard combinations of swear words that were brand new to some of us.

Teetering back on his heels, Mr. Guarancia took a couple of steps back, then lurched forward. He knew who the culprit was: Willie! He reached out and grabbed him with one hand by the front of his jacket and dragged the star pitcher toward the office. The other hand brushed away the orange juice, seeds, and bits of peel from his forehead. The rest of us stood silent, in shock and awe.

What just happened?

Although Mr. Guarancia was certain that Willie's arm was behind the orange missile, he hadn't actually seen it happen. So, he actually couldn't prove anything. And none of us in the boy's room had seen anything. "Too busy washing our hands, Sir." Willie, pleading the Fifth, was let go with the warning that "He would be watched closely."

The headache that Mr. G. suffered that afternoon must have been massive. And we did notice that after the orange smack in the noggin, he no longer took the same keen interest in catching smokers in the boy's room.

Well, Atchoo To You, Too!

Back in the day (the 1960s day) facial tissues (like Kleenex—the kind you blow your nose on and then throw away) were not common. No self-respecting guy would be walking around with a wad of Kleenex stuffed in his jeans. (Now some girls, especially those of the small breasted variety, might enhance their chests with a handful of tissues stuffed in a bra. Or use them, to remove makeup.)

Guys used handkerchiefs. Squares of hemmed white cotton that their mothers washed and hung up on the clothesline to dry on Mondays. Sometimes we called them "hankies," which I always thought was kind of prissy. But that's just me.

In the spring, during allergy season from early April through late May, all of us had a clean hankie every day. Sometimes more than one.

The Big House did not have air conditioning nor window screens, so the pollen was sucked through the open windows, drifted in waves through the halls, and later became trapped in the classrooms. Many kids, including yours truly, suffered through spring, hankie at the ready for the inevitable bouts of sneezes.

However, perhaps none of us suffered as much as Terry, the clean-cut flat-topped Kingston Trio disciple. Normally a fairly composed guy, he was the epitome of cool, until he was caught by an unexpected pollen wave and had to sneeze.

Terry was what is known as an "ugly, wet sneezer." That meant there was a wind-up phase that went in rising crescendo "ah! Ah! AH!" And then when the "CHOO part came, most of the copious (trying to be delicate here) fluid and gunk in Terry's nostrils, sinuses and brain pan came flying out at a great speed. The event was often compared to twin volcanoes erupting in unison.

So, now that you got that, let's move on to Terry's coolness—especially with girls. He fancied himself a bit of a studly.

Then there was the blonde—Sophia Loren. With a beautiful face, long hair, and a Coke bottle shape she completely intimidated almost every guy in NHS and, consequently, sat home alone on Saturday evenings because the guys were too chicken shit afraid to ask her out.

One more character. Kenny. Big gangly football player with hands as quick as lightning. Kenny is about to become Terry's former best friend. Did I tell you already that Kenny has a laugh like a demented banshee? Made the hair on your arms stand up straight and tall.

Both Kenny and Terry had a fondness for Sophia and

needled each other constantly about which one was the most chicken shit of all about asking her out.

Me? I'm just your humble observer and reporter of this little tableau.

We're on the second floor at NHS and Terry is walking toward his home room when he spots Sophia Loren, near the girl's room, walking toward him. Smiling.

Terry must have felt pretty confident about himself and walked right up to Miss Pretty Pants and started his love song. Not being close enough to overhear, I could only imagine what was being said, totally admiring what I was seeing. And the Blond Beauty seemed to be actually enjoying his performance.

Then it happened. A little springtime breeze, laden with pollen, crept up from behind. My eyes watered and nose tickled like Hell. I automatically reached for my hankie and sure enough the pollen count had just doubled with that little zephyr. I had all I could do to keep from sneezing my ass off and ruining the moment for the merry couple.

I continued watching the King of Smooth as he pulled out his spotless white hankie and lifted it toward his nose because the big sneeze was about to occur. He was already well into the "ah! Ah! AH!" stage and waiting to catch the mess in his hankie during "CHOO!" part.

Just then his big buddy, Kenny, comes running by and, like a flash, grabs that hankie right out of his hand.

As you know, there is no stopping what occurs when you are on the verge of a sneeze with your hankie on your nose. Like a nuclear reaction, once started, hankie or not, the sequence must be completed.

"CHOO!"

The Blond Beauty took one look at Terry (and his hand) and the last I saw of her she was going into the girl's room and looking quite ill herself.

Kenny was tumbling down the hall, laughing like a rabid hyena, holding the spotless handkerchief aloft like a trophy flag. Terry had turned and was cussing out Kenny like a trooper.

When the vice principal found out about the incident, he called both Terry and Kenny to the office. Even he laughed and ordered the two to shake hands.

"Not 'til I'm sure he washed them," Kenny protested.

Sophia Loren avoided both of them for the next few days.

Both of them remained chicken shit and never asked her out.

Terry and Kenny are still friends to this day. And in the spring Terry's handkerchief, held securely in two hands, still gets a good work out every day.

The Lemonade Hour

Most of our teachers at NHS were old (probably north of 40), tired and not much fun. But there were rare exceptions.

Miss Eagles was one of them. She was young, attractive, well-dressed, a bit forward, and fresh out of college. So not more than two or three years older than some of our career 12th graders. She had an apartment in a building near the school and in good weather she walked to NHS and home again. For bad weather she had a little, red foreign car that belched blue smoke and obviously burned oil.

Most people, especially most of the guys, if they were walking behind her would slow down. Speed up if they were ahead. You didn't walk with a teacher no matter how young and attractive they were. Especially if they were young and attractive.

If you did, everyone knew that you were kissing ass to get a better grade. And that wasn't cool. Or maybe you had more personal thoughts.

In this day and age Maddy Eagles would probably be fired, prosecuted, and jailed for even walking with a student. But, as they say in the Acme Ginsu Knife ads, "There's more."

The few guys who walked with her often carried her books. Of course, they were heavy! If it was raining and one of them was on foot, she would often stop and give them a lift. Such a sweetheart.

Occasionally (we were told) she would invite one of the guys in for some lemonade. They must have been very thirsty carrying all of those heavy books. Uphill, too. Did it take close to an hour to drink a lemon aide? I rather doubt that.

Of course, what went on behind closed doors has stayed exactly that way for close to sixty years. So, we'll never know for sure, but it all makes for a titillating story.

Miss (no "Ms." back then) Eagles was also known to be a bit of a bully, at least for some students. Like Cory Maitland.

Cory was a good student who did as little as humanly possible to maintain average grades and float along quietly. Besides, studying inferred with his active social life that included the usual girls, cars, beer, cigarettes, and Saturday nights at the drive-in.

But Miss Eagles took a dislike to him. (Maybe she knew that he suspected the lemonade afternoons involved more than a cold drink.) Her favorite pursuit was having him read, aloud, from *A Tale of Two Cities*. You know the one: "It was the best of times. It was the worst of times." by Charles Dickens, written in the year and language of 1859. With lots of French names and words.

Cory hated being the butt of the teacher's little joke, reading aloud in front of the class, stumbling over the unfamiliar words, and English literature—in that order.

So, he just gave up. The next time Miss E. asked him to read aloud from the dreaded book he ignored her.

"You can either read aloud from the book or go to the Vice Principal's office," was the ultimatum. Cory was gone from the classroom in a New York second.

At NHS Vice Principal Everett Baker was in charge of discipline and his waiting room was usually overflowing.

He was tough and strict, but fair. When his turn before Mr. Baker arrived Cory carefully and patiently described the situation.

"He was," he explained, "being harassed and embarrassed for no apparent reason other than for the enjoyment of Miss Eagles."

The Vice Principal addressed the situation with kid gloves, gave Cory a good talking to, a few detentions, and got a promise that he would behave and do as he was told if Miss Eagles asked him to do something.

"Okay, deal done!" Cory agreed with his fingers crossed behind his back.

Now you have to know this. Miss Eagle's classroom had big bookshelves at the back that had multiple copies of all of the books that the class would use over the year. That way students didn't have to buy their own copy.

There were probably 30 copies of "Tale." Then there were none!

Overnight they had all disappeared, never to be found again.

Rumor had it that the football team got together and decided to help out one of their buddies.

Even more strange: Not one single word was ever said about the missing books and Cory, who had chosen the Vice Principal's office over reading aloud, was never questioned about them.

My vision is that someday, a few thousand years from now, some archaeologist will be digging through the

Norwalk City Dump and find 30 copies of Dicken's book all in a pile. Then he or she will compose a learned, but speculative, paper about how that all came to be.

Mother Gray

Back in the late 50s/early 60s we didn't really know much about homosexuals. We called them "queers" and there was a lot of whispering, most of it hearsay. Of course, Norwalk was close to New York City and we "knew" that there were "many queers" among the music, acting, and artistic communities. But in Norwalk, it wasn't something you put on everyday public display.

The exception was the NHS librarian, Mr. Gray. Or as we called him, "Mother Gray."

Now, in case you think we were all "anti-gay bigots" you have to take into account the times.

Let me paint this scenario.

It was the late 1950s. Many of our fathers were World War II veterans who had seen the horrors of war and most seldom, or never, talked about it. The economy was booming. The Cold War was in full swing. Authorities told us to shelter under our desks if a nuclear attack took place during school hours. Senator Eugene McCarthy had just finished finding Communists everywhere amongst us. The most popular country song in October 1958 was *Squaws Along the Yukon are Good Enough for Me.* True. Look it up on YouTube.

The idea of 'political correctness' was still somewhere off in the future.

Adults didn't talk about heterosexual sex (especially to their kids), let alone homosexual sex. Sex was something to be closeted. Girls were "expected" to remain virgins until marriage. Boys were given a bit more latitude, but if you got a girl in a "family way" her father might paint his shotgun white to ensure a formal wedding.

So, harassing Mr. Gray was just part of the scenery of the times. And the way he reacted guaranteed return engagements a few times a year.

Mr. Gray was, as we might term it today, a 'flamer.' Very effeminate in his demeanor, walked with a swish, wore pink shirts and shoes with bows and flowers, and reeked of perfume (not aftershave). Of course, there were the limp wrists and hissy speech.

He was the school librarian and ran the place like a prison—enter quietly, quickly take a seat, speak only when spoken to. Otherwise, you were (very quietly) to leave and not come back.

Here's the geography! There was a boy's room on each of the three floors of the school. The one on the first floor faced the library. In early September it was warm and most of the windows were open. So, a few jokers would enter the boy's room on the library side of the school, crowd into the window and scream out: "MOTHER GRAY! GOT SOMETHING FOR YOU!"

Of course, the boys, thinking this was the height of good fun, were laughing so hard they almost fell over each other trying to get out of the boys' room and back into the hall.

There they would wait and watch, out of sight, as Mother Gray came flying across from the library and up the steps toward the boys' room, charging full blast into the now-empty stalls, looking for his tormenters.

Mr. Gray could have saved himself a lot of hassle if he had ignored the catcalls from the boy's room, but that didn't seem to be in his character. As for the perps, they never seemed to get caught.

A Few Extra Years

Larry D. was a fine young man who thought so much of NHS that he stayed for a few extra years. I asked him why he was still in NHS and he said he loved it in school and enjoyed the social fun stuff.

Wow, just when we thought everyone wanted to get out on their own, he volunteers for three more years! Hell, he was twenty-one years old when he decided it was time to leave. He had good grades but always dropped a few classes and never had enough credits to graduate. So, he did what no one else ever did or wanted to do. He stayed until he felt it was his time to leave! Go figure that one out folks and find out what he says.

Anyway, he had a beautiful '58 Chevy convertible painted Candy Apple Red with several custom items done. It was low, had a Corvette grille, a 348 engine, three deuces, and dual exhaust. He also always had a smile on his face and a pretty girl at his side.

The Body In The Trunk

Cars, beer, girls, and the occasional State Trooper made our lives complete.

Occasionally one of the elements was missing. This time it was 'girls.'

It was just before graduation and we all had a serious case of that kids today call "the fuckits;" when you know that you're going to graduate anyway, so long as you don't commit a class one felony, so why do any work?

A bunch of us decided we needed a few beers and a pizza. So, we piled into my '58 Chevy Impala convertible, picked up Crotchy at Swanky Franks, and cruised on down the New England Turnpike toward New York.

Just as an aside, the Turnpike eventually became I-95, making it all the way down to Hemingway's house in Florida—with the other end somewhere in the north. Since none of us ever went past Boston (why would you?) we never found out where the northern terminus was. Maybe in a snowbank in Maine?

Anyway, there we were, doing the exact speed limit,

top up, sipping the last of our beer. There were a few toll plazas before our exit at Portchester, and we didn't want open beer in the car. I had cut a very discreet slit in the convertible cover so we could slip the empties into the trunk. Very handy for leaving the Drive-In or the beach.

Of course, you never know what's going to happen next. In this case the trunk lid popped open. The trunk lid on that car was about the size of a barn door and on springs that could lift a battleship. It stood straight up in the air like a huge turquoise wall making the car unstable and cutting off the rearview vision. Traffic was heavy, moving at 60, and we were in the middle lane. Pulling over and stopping wasn't a good option.

"Crotchy, crawl through the hole into the trunk and pull the lid down," I yelled.

"Screw you," was Crotchy's response.

"No. It's OK. Someone grab his legs and hold on to him."

Crotchy wiggles and squirms into the trunk and is just about to reach up to pull the trunk lid down when an old lady following us is sure she sees "a body in the trunk," hits the brakes, changes lanes, and peels off onto an exit to report it to the police. (Of course, we find all of this out later from the State Trooper who will eventually enter the story.)

With the trunk lid down, we continue on to the Square Tavern, drank 10-cent drafts and had a cheap pizza. I remember we even had a round of Crab Orchard Whiskey in celebration of our upcoming graduation. Crab Orchard is gut-rot, no one drank it unless you were getting over a bad breakup. But it was cheap. And for most of us, well, we were only going to graduate once.

We drove home up Route 1, through the little towns, checking out the girls and action. No hurry. Stopped at a White Tower to pee and empty out the beer cans. No hurry.

Next thing you know we're being run down by a State Trooper with siren blasting and lights flashing. He gets out with his weapon drawn. Holy shit! Then two Darrien cops come flying up the road with everything screaming and flashing and stop in front of us. Did we unknowingly commit a class one felony? Would this mean we wouldn't graduate after all?

The Trooper tells us to stay in the car, hands on the wheel or otherwise placed where they can be seen and stay still.

Eventually the whole story came out. The trunk lid popping up. Crotchy's exit. The old lady seeing the body. After all, this was Mafia and gangster country, so a report of seeing a body in a trunk was not to be discounted in any way.

They called the Square Tavern, and someone confirmed that we'd been there. (Which goes to show that drinking and driving was considered a much less serious offense than transporting a dead body in the trunk of a car.)

We even showed the Trooper the hole into the trunk. He was impressed. Of course, there were no beer cans, which was also good.

The Troopers had called my parents after they traced the car tag number, so I had some detailed explanations to take care of when I got home.

We laughed a lot about it later. And we all graduated from NHS. Most of us for the first and last time.

CHAPTER THREE

Hot Wheels

Just Some Guys Looking for a Race

In our world in the '50s, a car became a hot rod when the owner started to personalize his ride. He might lower the car, put on glass pack mufflers to give it a nice mellow tone, Then, of course, special wheel covers (aka hubcaps), white walls, and perhaps, a John Kurtzman pinstripe job on the dash, vent windows and (Wow!) a name on the side of the front fenders.

In the early days, most kids had an old Ford. They were cheap, plentiful, and easy to work on. Parts were interchangeable among different years.

Then came the early Chevy V-8's in the mid-50s. Plenty of interchangeable, cheap parts. And their low weight compared to the competition meant they were also fast.

How fast? Well, that depended on whom and where

you were racing.

The Boston Post Road went through the center of Norwalk, north to the Westport town line and south to the Darien town line. In between were 20 miles of traffic lights where the boys sized up the competition.

A couple of hot rod drivers might meet at a red light, exchange hard glances, and then peel off on green to test out the other, letting off the gas before the cops took interest.

It was a short "getting to know ya" event.

If there was a good match up, the drivers might move on to the entrance of Route 95, aka "the local drag strip."

95 was a good strip. The State Troopers had a lot of area to cover. Much of the highway had a three-foot metal barrier running down the median, and few places to turn around.

The two racers would line up on the highway and the passenger in the right front of the outside car would start the count. "One. Two. Three Go!"

Wham! Hammer down! Through the gears. If a driver was winning he might start to back off at 80; if he was losing he might jack it up to 100 or, if losing badly, lift his foot around 60 to 70.

In any event, the whole thing was over in 15 seconds or so. Even if the Troopers saw the race, by the time they got turned around and caught up again, there were a few guys in hot rods tooling along just under the speed limit. One driver would have a wide smile.

The "championship" moved among many hotrodders over time. It was kind of like gunslingers in the Old West. There was always somebody coming down the road who was faster than you. And keeping a hotrod in race-winning shape took time, money, and talent.

Like having two girlfriends at the same time in the same town—eventually one won. And usually, the car lost to the real girl. The cars gathered dust, got sold off, and emerged at 'Cruise In' nights piloted by old guys trying to rediscover their lost youth.

The "factory rods" from Chevrolet, Ford, and others in the '60s were the final nail in the DIY hotrodder's coffin. Of course, there were a few brave hearts who would race against the factory-builts, but it was a losing game.

By 1965 it was all but over for the true hotrodder, unless he bought a 55 Chevy and installed the latest, greatest factory high horsepower engine, added a four-speed transmission, a good ratio rear end, and a big set of tires.

A guy could save all that effort and expense and just buy the factory car direct. Most of them were faster than anything he could build anyway.

The Last Race—With Two Winners

While the home grown hotrodders held sway over the measured three-quarter mile and the tracks, there were some were some prime vehicles.

The '53 Ford built by George Daon was finished in a never-to-be-painted off-gray primer. While the car was not particularly fast, it was very cool with a Buick engine, big old Caddy floor shift transmission, and a set of sticky, wide tires on the back to give it extra grab.

Another unique custom car was built by a guy named McGurik. He started out with a 1934 green two-door Studebaker convertible with a rumble seat and spare tires in the front fenders. He added wide white wall tires, a giant three-carburetor Olds engine that sat high on the frame, a new transmission, and a lot of chrome. McGurik painted it candy apple red.

John Tarnowski bought it, street raced it a few times, and pronounced it "fast!" Then, during one race, the accelerator stuck to the floor and, rumor has it, the pedal released when the car was topping out at 125. Tarnowski sold the body and kept the engine which later turned up in a lighter 1940 black primer Ford Coupe.

Another black primer Ford coupe with a big Buick engine lived up the road in Westport was owned by a guy named Lasorda. He and Tarnowski were to meet up for a big race later in the year. But Tarnowski fell in love (with a girl) and sold his coupe to musician Lionel Chamberland, a man who never showed fear (except when surrounded by cows, as we will learn later).

Lionel took up the challenge and the race was set for the I-95 right across from Swanky Franks. It was a natural quarter mile raceway which was, from bridge to bridge, a quarter of a mile, compliments of the Highway Department.

Bob "Crotchy" Crochetiere was the official starter. A friend in a semi stopped traffic out on the highway for the few seconds the race would take. Crotchy, ahead and in between the coupes would point to one car, make sure it was ready, the same with the other, then jump into the air signaling the start.

The '40 Ford coupes were identical (remember that, it's important) exhausts bypassing the mufflers, tire pressure low for extra traction. Each driver was alone (to keep the weight down) holding the gear shift tightly, one foot lightly holding the clutch, revving the engine with the other. Kids from Norwalk and Westport crowding together on the bridge, jostling for the best view.

Crotchy leapt into the air. The race of the year began.

The ear-splitting exhaust drowned out the engine noise and screaming tires. Then you could hear the engines shriek as they reached for second and the headlights leaped toward the dark sky for a split second as the duo shot under the bridge.

They continued side by side through the smoke and noise with the Norwalk and Westport supporters watching.

It soon dawned on us that we didn't know which car was which—they both looked the same. (I told you that was important to remember.)

You could see the rear ends of the cars jerk a bit from side to side as the drivers shifted into third and the sound soon changed as both drivers let off the gas. Flames shot out of the pipes as the gas in the throats of the beasts burned.

Then they were gone, fearing that they would be caught for racing or driving with open exhausts. Lasorda took the beach road back to Westport; Lionel headed back to Norwalk as quietly as possible and locked up his car in the garage.

From our perch on the bridge we could see the flashing lights speeding up the Boston Post Road. We all melted away into the night, each side confident that their guy had won.

It was an epic race for a number of reasons. Both cars had won, and the drivers never revealed what they knew—or didn't know about the outcome. No one got a ticket; a significant bonus.

And the race really signaled the end of the custom hotrod era, although we didn't realize it at the time. The factory-builts were the real winners after that night.

Midnight Shopping

When you have a car (that you want to work on) and not a lot of money, you have to be creative. Especially when it comes to procuring those extra special items (read: expensive) for your beloved car.

Such was the case for any number of teenagers all across America back in the day. And, of course, in Norwalk, CT.

One way was to go to your local auto wrecking yards. Maybe you called them "junk yards." In any case, the sheer quantity of scrapped, wrecked, and incomplete vehicles was truly staggering. Here you could probably find almost any part from almost any car.

Our wrecking yards happened to be side by side in lower south Norwalk. They were owned by French Canadian families: the LaJoie family and the LeBlanc family.

(There were several French Canadian families in Norwalk including the Chamberlands and the Crotchetieres.)

Both families had a couple of sons who went to school at NHS with us. Don LaJoie became very successful as a stock car racer throughout Connecticut, and was eventually inducted into the New England Auto Racing Hall of Fame.

His son, Randy, became a household name racing NASCAR for several years. Both Casey and Cory LaJoie, Randy's sons, are making left turns for a living with

NASCAR, and I'm quite sure all of Norwalk is rooting them on.

The LeBlanc family was also very active in the local car scene. Their sons had two exceptional cars: quality restorations of '57 Chevys which would later become the iconic legendary car of the '50s and are high dollar cars to this day. The LeBlanc brothers branched out into real estate as the years rolled on.

Anyway, if you paid a visit to their junk yards back then, anything could be found but, could you afford to purchase the item? Well, most times you couldn't, so something else had to be done. Yes, my friends, you might consider liberating it from the junk yard!

But, you've heard of junk yard dogs. The two junk yards in south Norwalk let their man-eating dogs run loose in the yards at night so a midnight visit was out of the question.

Now, if it were just a set of fancy hub caps you desired, you could ride around until you saw the ones you wanted and stake out the location. By that I mean see how dark it was, the traffic, or were they getting food to go (which meant they would be back soon). All this was very important.

Or, another option, you could go to another junk yard out of town (which maybe didn't have vicious dogs running loose at night) and case the place. A bit of thoughtful wandering in the event that the owners or staff were watching: "Oh look, there's what I want over there—so keep walking and we'll stop over there and pretend we're really interested in the '49 Lincoln generator." Later, the car guy in need ventured forth with the necessary tools, ready to do a little moonlight shopping.

Such a place was Danbury, which had a very big junk yard and dogs which were tied up. They could bark, but they couldn't bite! By the light of the silvery moon the getaway car was parked at a convenient place not too far down the road. Over the fence, as quietly as possible, the desperadoes would sneak toward their chosen aisle and commence liberating.

But lo and behold, there were cows walking around inside the junk yard.

Now who would have thought it? Cows in a junk yard? Can't be much for them to eat there.

And, who would have thought it? One of the intrepid intruders—Link Chamberland—the coolest, most unflinching, "I spit at danger, I laugh at 125 miles an hour," was deathly afraid of cows. I mean, he could faint in the presence of plain, old milk cows. The stupidest, least dangerous large animals on earth.

So, in the midst of this midnight shopping expedition with cows, there was tough guy Link making child-like whimpering noises and waving his arms like a windmill.

Well, that started a minor cattle stampede for a minute. Then the dogs started barking full throat. House and yard lights flicked on. But, the guys came for parts, and they were not leaving until they liberated them.

The curious cows became quite interested in what was

going on and stayed close. They continued to be a problem for the tough-guy-crybaby who wasn't much help in the shopping department.

Then, suddenly, the dogs were let loose, the shopping was completed, and the society of midnight shoppers were in full flight toward the getaway car.

Fortunately, the car started on the first crank and once the last door was slammed shut, the driver went as fast as he could (with no lights) for a few hundred yards, so the owners who were following the dogs could not get a good look the intruder's ride.

Link, the "man-boy cow-boy," took a lot of ribbing about his aversion to bovines in the night. Which he did not take that well.

The "new" parts looked good and performed magnificently in their new location. That moonlight shopping adventure was the subject of much retelling over the years (with the appropriate embellishments). And, of course, the price was right.

Afternoon Shopping

Midnight shopping for car parts was relatively safe and easy. You nonchalantly picked out the part(s) you wanted/ needed at a junk yard, wandered around for a bit longer as if you were just browsing to throw off suspicion, and left. Under the cover of darkness, and with the appropriate tools in hand, you revisited said junk yard and, quickly and quietly, liberated the part(s).

Speed was of the essence, of course. A rusted bolt or balky fitting would slow down the process. The dogs would set up a hue and cry, the owner or watchman would turn them loose, and the midnight shopping spree would be over. It was run for it, into the waiting dark car, turn the key hoping that you didn't flood the engine or jump the clutch, and off down some country road with no lights in the dark. No problem.

Afternoon shopping? Well, that added a whole new dimension to the activity. You had to do the deed in full view in daylight. That took brass balls and total confidence that you could do the job. Quickly!

This story concerns just such an undertaking: To acquire a very particular starter motor from a very nice car on a busy side street. Of course, it was available at a junk yard, but was very expensive to buy as a traditional cash transaction. The starter in question was from a Cadillac, usually impossible to liberate through the midnight shopping technique; the junk yards would remove the pricey part from the discarded hulk and keep it in their parts shop behind the counter.

Our heroes are Charlie and John. It takes two for afternoon shopping: The brass-balled surgeon, John, to slip unnoticed under the car with sturdy instruments and a bag to hold and hide the newly acquired part from prying eyes. Charlie, the lookout, to lean casually against the fender, checking his nails and watching the passing clouds, or reading the sports section to keep up with the Yankees.

After spotting the donor Caddy, the boys watched for over a week, noting the times of coming and going. (There is a time investment needed for afternoon shopping!) The owner, they discovered was a man of habit.

On the appointed day the owner returned from lunch, parked the car on the usual side street, ran his hand over the chromed tail fin, and went back to work. Charlie and John waited long enough for the car to cool off (no benefit in burning the surgeon's hands) and then sauntered over. John quickly disappeared underneath like a ghost in a graveyard. Charlie leaned casually against the fender, as if waiting for the owner to return momentarily, glowering over the latest exploits of the damn Yankees.

The mailman came by, said "Hi," to Charlie and stopped as if to chat. But the day was overcast, and a fortuitous drizzle set in which helped hurry the mailman along. Underneath the car, John resumed breathing as Charlie whispered "OK. He's gone," and folded up his wet paper.

About three minutes later John rolled out, stood up smoothly, and the two sauntered off about their business, a heavy bag firmly in John's grip. His hands were clean and there was not a spot of grease on his checked shirt. Charlie shook out a Camel for John and himself. They lit up and continued on as if they had all day.

The owner, a heavyset and excitable Italian gentleman, returned to his car after work, climbed in and turned the key anticipating, no doubt, pasta and gravy, this being a Thursday. Nothing. Just a distant click from somewhere under the hood. Repeated attempts yielded the same result.

Slamming the door, the owner hiked off to the nearest gas station and returned with a mechanic who opened the hood, peered in, checked the battery, and then settled himself behind the wheel. Nothing, as he turned the key.

Back under the hood the mechanic discovered the dangling wire that should be connected to the starter motor, which seemed to be missing in action. Under the car the mechanic confirmed his suspicions: No starter motor. This was tough to explain to the owner.

"Where's my fucking starter motor?" the pissed off owner demanded.

"Well," the mechanic rubbed his stubbly cheek. "It could have fallen off as you were driving back from lunch," he said.

"Are you fucking nuts? I would have heard it fall off."

"Well, maybe. Maybe not," was the mechanic's opinion. "Or," he offered an alternative scenario, "someone wanted that starter motor more than you and removed it from the car here this afternoon."

There was a lot of cursing and swearing in Italian, English and other languages. "How do I get another starter motor?'

Back at the service station the mechanic made a few calls, however the auto parts distributors were closing (by now it was 6:00 pm), but they could have it at the service station first thing in the morning. Cost: $100.

More Italian fireworks that the service station manager helped to quench with four fingers of Scotch left over from a mild winter.

"So, how do I get home?" the Italian asked wiping the last drop of Scotch from his chin.

No one was very familiar with the owner's part of town, the part with big homes and bigger lawns, so one of the juniors was appointed to be chauffeur and away they went.

Much like the end of "The Night Before Christmas" we could hear him exclaim all manner of things in various languages as they drove out of sight, but "Merry Christmas to all" was not on the list.

Some People Were Meant to Go Fast

I can't let the fast car and cool driver stories go without a mention of a few other people.

Ray Cummings

Ray Cummings was a brilliant young man who had the bad luck to grow up with a bunch of juvenile delinquents as friends. By the time he was a preteen he discovered he was smart and, while he hung around his juvenile delinquent friends when it suited him, he was on the dean's list in school. He was also a hotrodder.

After graduating from Tufts University with a Master's in engineering, he treated himself to a loaded, built-for-drag-racing, '62 Corvette. He raced it on the streets and did rather well.

Although Ray was brilliant, he lacked certain fundamentals, AKA common sense. So, he was quite surprised when, after only 5,000 miles of street racing, the 'Vette needed a new set of tires. His former friends could have, no doubt, warned him, and given a moonless night, could have supplied him with a brand new (gently worn) set of replacements.

Having a positraction rear end on your hotrod was a real benefit. It meant that it was pretty well impossible to spin the wheels and lose the grip on the road, especially from a standing stop at a traffic light or on the track.

Imagine a new 64 Chevy Impala 409 with a 435 horsepower four-speed and a posi rear end. Straight from the factory. With a warranty. Fred Farnam had one.

Since he just happened to be the son of a millionaire, Fred was never hurting for money, but he was always just one of the guys who wanted to have fun. Which he did with his Chevy 409, until he accidently impregnated a girlfriend. Although he often summered on Martha's Vineyard, he spent the next 40 years working full time at Uncle Joe's Restaurant while driving boring family sedans. Karma (or "Car-ma") is a bitch.

Joe Azery, Phil Orrico, and our friend, Officer Fredericks

Some of the guys who built hotrods were considered semi-crazy, or crazy like a fox, depending on your point of view.

Joe Azery was the only guy I knew to chop his own convertible—a bright yellow '41 Ford. He cut five inches off the front windshield post and replaced the factory windshield and rear window with smaller, but legal, glass, so it had a seven-inch-high windshield. Doing all of this didn't make the car any faster, (it already had a big Buick engine) but it made it look one hell of lot meaner.

Then there are two others who are an integral part of this story. First was Phil Orrico who had a '59 Chevy Impala that was hot off the green light. The final actor in our little drama was the Norwalk cop that most guys lived to hate: Officer Fredericks.

One fine evening Joe (in his chopped '41 Ford) and Phil (in his '59 Chevy) were fooling around on the Boston Post Road—peeling out, making noise and slamming gears—generally just having fun and hanging out.

Enter Officer Fredericks who pulls a U-turn and goes after Joe with siren blaring and lights flashing. Phil did his best to get in the way while Joe turned off his lights, floored the big Buick engine, and ran for home.

Later that same evening, when me, Phil, and Lionel Chamberland arrived at Joe's he was busily painting his formerly yellow car with a fresh coat of dark primer. The very next day Joe was off to the Motor Vehicle office to get a new registration for his car—which listed the vehicle's color as "dark gray."

Joe stayed off the road for a few weeks until the new

paint smell had dissipated and then let himself be stopped by our old pal Officer Fredericks, who accused him of racing on the street and then escaping.

"What kind of car were you looking for," Joe asked innocently.

Officer Fredericks read from his little notebook: "A hotrod car, color yellow, northbound at a high rate of speed."

"Hmmm," Joe mused. "See, you say 'yellow,' but my car here is dark gray. Look at my registration. It clearly says, 'Dark Gray.'"

Officer Fredericks was not happy. Joe was pleased. Crazy like a fox.

One footnote to the story: Phil's '59 Chevy engine blew up one night as he was besting some other driver, so a new one was in order.

One of the rules of hotrodding was that you could not replace any part with a lesser part. So that Impala 283 became a 348 power pack, later to have triple carbs. He now had a 315 horsepower monster versus the paltry 230 it replaced.

His car was so fast he could catch any girl he wanted, and often did. Then one day Phil traded in his beloved wheels and was soon married. He had obviously chased down a girl who wanted to be caught.

Rick Setti
Rick Setti's dad bought a new Pontiac with the biggest

engine available, a 389 cubic inch baby putting out 300 wild horses. Dual exhausts, floor shift, and positraction completed the package.

Rick tore the tires off it in less than 60 days or 5,000 miles which caused his father some upset. But you have to understand, there were a zillion traffic lights along the Boston Post Road, and guys like Rick firmly believed that you had to peel away from every one of them as if you were in a drag race for your life.

Along with many others, Rick's glory days centered around Norwalk High School where he was a star third base player all three years. Had he been a better hitter, he might have been called up for the big show. But he got married right out of high school and was a proud father a few months later.

Jane English

Hotrodding was mostly an activity for guys, but there were a few ladies who stood out, especially Miss Jane English. She was a one-of-a-kind who was smart in school, a golden-haired beauty with a lead foot, good hand-eye coordination, and fearlessness, or will, and "drive" to win to be a champion hotrodder.

Our local Dover Drag Strip in Wingate, NY held a Power Puff Race Day every month just for the ladies. Jane won trophies more often than she lost, but her family never knew it.

Her father disapproved of smart girls who could drive a hotrod to victory and loved to drink beer. So, we took photos of her with the day's trophies, and then traded them in for beer at our favorite watering hole.

She did end up with a nice car, courtesy of her father. He had been in Miami on business and drove back a bright red, two-door, '59 Impala with a 348 engine and a standard shift, presenting it to her with some fanfare.

He didn't realize how good she was and remained unaware of the vast amounts of rubber she left at the traffic lights on the Boston Post Road as she outperformed most of the competition. Having a ride this great also made her even more popular with the guys, but she had told several of the most persistent that she was saving herself for marriage. Which, as far as I know, she did.

Miss Jane enjoyed her Impala throughout the summer and into the cooler fall days in Norwalk when she found a problem. Walking into the B&T one October day she announced that the heater wasn't working and could we have a look. Instantly there were five guys all under the hood and under the dash of her car. All five guys then announced that the car didn't have a heater. There was a space where it should be, but it wasn't there.

Her dad came down to inspect, suspecting (I believe) that the guys from the B&T were trying to (figuratively) screw over his beautiful teenage daughter with the equally beautiful car.

Well, he admitted after taking a closer look, who would have thought that a car from Miami wouldn't have a heater? We ordered the parts and installed a heater to keep her warm and cozy through the long Norwalk winter.

Ballad of the Henry J

Mike DiScala was just starting his career in Real Estate (he later became a household name in the Norwalk area) when he got the hotrod bug. He was joined by his cousin, Sal Grillo.

Sal had a cream-colored Kaiser Frazer, a convertible Italian sports car with red interior which he only drove in nice weather. No wonder. The car is so rare that its worth a quarter of a million dollars.

Neither Mike nor Sal knew very much in the way of working on cars, nor could they diagnosis what could possibly be wrong when it did not function the way it was supposed to. But a little problem like that didn't stop them.

When it came time to picking a potential race car, they both decided on the "Henry J," which were both plentiful and very cheap. There was a reason for this. They were cheaply made, fell apart rapidly, and owners got rid of them quickly.

Henry J's were very light, just a little over 2,000 pounds, and you wanted a light car combined with a lot of power to make it go as fast as possible.

I'm not sure who actually assembled the car, but it had the best of everything in it. Unfortunately for Mike and Sal, it never performed as expected (although it sounded really fast!) and the cousins moved on.

Cars with a Special Purpose:
Building a Better Drag Car

During my time growing up in Norwalk there were two purpose built drag cars. The fastest one was built by my brother, John, driven by my friend Paul Fusco, and sponsored by the B&T Texaco.

The only purpose for a drag car was to go from a dead stop and through a measured quarter mile as fast as possible. These cars looked kind of like the ordinary street cars, not today's rail-like top fuelers with gigantic rear tires that go so fast they need parachutes to help them get stopped at the finish line.

Because a purpose build car (like a drag car) is so exotic, it has to be planned meticulously in advance and a "build sheet" created that lists all of the components in detail and how they will be put together. The builder has to consider whether the completed car will blow up, vibrate to death, or otherwise self-destruct. The life and welfare of the builder, mechanics and driver have to be considered. Not to mention the spectators who might be injured if the vehicle comes apart or leaves the track at 100+ miles an hour.

The builder might start with, say, a '37 Ford coupe. By the time they were finished, about the only original part left was the sheet metal body.

An engine capable of producing high horsepower would be selected, taken apart, and completely rebuilt with specially made racing parts: new camshaft, newly milled heads, high compression pistons, bigger valves, hotter ignition, bigger and more carburetors, custom exhaust, and so on.

Then everything had to be balanced: engine, fly wheel, clutch, transmission, rear end and drive shaft—to ensure that one component didn't tear apart another one.

Brakes were critical—you had to restrain the monster from 110+ miles an hour to full stop space in a very short space—one-eighth of a mile at the most.

Fuel was also a big consideration. Ordinary B&T Texaco from the pump was not going to make it. We needed a lot more oomph if we were going to take home the hardware.

We tried many different combinations such as alcohol mixed with Amoco hi-test, Sunoco 280 (one of the highest octane ratings available) mixed with acetone, and a combination of Texaco with Sunoco 280. High octane airplane gas allowed the builder to put more timing into the engine. It was difficult to buy, not owning an airplane, but sometimes we scored.

Of course, we were dealing with very volatile high explosives which could easily blow up or otherwise destroy a great and expensive engine. Or the building. Or us. Or all of the above.

In the end we settled on Texaco hi-test and, perhaps, a little secret sauce as giving us the most power without the danger of blowing up the neighborhood.

We fastened a five-gallon Moon tank on the front of the car where the front bumper should be with feed lines to the two very hi-tech four-barrel carbs.

The driver would start the engine with regular gasoline and, when the time came, pull a knob that would allow the exotic mixture to fuel the engine. Usually there were only two possibilities: the car went terrifyingly fast, or it stalled and/or blew up.

This was a lockable tank. It would take only a few seconds for someone to slip something into the tank that would sabotage our day. When the racing was over, we emptied the tank, wiped the inside and cleaned out the lines. Otherwise, the gas had a tendency to turn into something like varnish and clog up everything.

Drag racing also taught us a valuable life lesson. Like airplane pilots, we had a check list for almost everything, including end-of-race-day shut down. One person completed the tasks and another person double checked to make sure they were done correctly. Some called us "anal," but we won consistently, never broke anything, and the neighborhood still stands. Some of our competitors could not make the same claim.

The Interior Built for Speed (not luxury!)

Inside the drag car, practicality is the main and only

feature.

Builders chose the Spartan way: If you really need it, get the best. But keep it simple; only what is necessary to make the driver better and the car faster.

There is the legal, NHRA-approved race car seat, welded in place to make it as sturdy and solid as possible. The National Hot Rod Association-approved roll cage, constructed and installed according to strict instructions. If your car should become airborne at over 100 mph, roll a few times, bounce around, spin and came to rest on the roof, a good roll cage would be handy to have.

Other safety and security additions like seat belts, shoulder harness, fire extinguisher, and helmet all had to meet NHRA spec, or you would fail inspection and be sent home with a helpful to-do list to complete if you wanted to race again in a sanctioned event.

And absolutely no loose items that might become lethal missiles if things went bad at a high speed. If there was dust or small particulate inside the car it would rise up like fog after 80 mph, and then settle back to the floor when the driver let off the gas. The answer was to use the vacuum cleaner before the race to suck up all of these minute UFOs.

Oddly, the rules did not include having the "necessary" gauges like temperature, an accurate oil gauge, and a tachometer. The tach sat directly in front of the driver so that he did not have to turn his head or even move his eyes to read the RPMs. The tach is THE gauge. It tells the driver when to shift.

The team practices for hours to determine the exact RPM when the engine is putting out maximum power in every gear—usually between 6,000 and 7,500 RPM. The driver strategy is to push the engine to get maximum power (as shown on the tach) out of every gear, then shift to the next gear and do the same. With a millisecond to power shift—depress the clutch, move the shift lever, release the clutch with the accelerator hard on the floor all the time—at the exact second the tach show the max RPM requires great hand-eye-foot coordination and a lot of nerve. Being a nano second slow, or fast, would result in a big bang, a very quiet engine, a big cloud of oily smoke, and an expensive rebuild back at the shop.

The Fastest Car in Norwalk

The B&T Texaco car was the fastest Norwalk ever had and, in their day, Fusco and the car had a decent following. It was well deserved.

My brother John did his work meticulously and his build sheet was strong. Fusco and the car were kind of married to each other. They knew what the other liked and seemed to have great respect for each other. As a consequence, nothing broke and together they won races.

Back then a hotrod running in the mid-12 seconds for the quarter mile was considered fast, and the B&T coupe was well in that area. That would put it at 108-112 miles per hour when Fusco hit the brakes and eased off.

That may seem easy—12 seconds of work—but there was a lot of physical and mental effort packed into those few seconds. Just getting the car off the line was dangerous and required exacting timing; the clutch throw was perhaps an inch and stalling out with an engine at max RPM was a very distinct possibility. There were three power shifts during the 12 seconds of terror. And just keeping the vehicle on the straight (and narrow) required great strength and experience as the monster handled differently with every few miles an hour of increased speed, at some points threatening to become airborne. Stopping was as much of an art as a science and included everything short of throwing out an anchor.

A few additional semi-power shifts at the finish line helped to slow and stop the beast.

Keeping the car running at top performance required hours of delicate tuning and tinkering by brother John between racing weekends. And that required "testing" to determine if the adjustments made a difference.

There was a routine and a route.

Either Paul or I would fire up the creature and let it idle to get warm. Put together a high-power engine with no muffler and the noise was earsplitting. Just the initial "WHAP!" of the ignition would wake up every dog in the area, and signal to every housewife hanging out the wash, that the Awakening was about to take place.

The test road took us up Route 123 (straight as a giant oak in the forest) toward New Canaan at a sedate 70 to 80 miles per hour, blasting the paint off the other cars as we shot past them.

Then take an exit, perform a noisy turn-around in a driveway, then explode back south to the B&T where we'd debrief our leader on the car's performance, pop a beer or three, and giggle about how much fun we were having.

Strangely, the police never bothered us during our assaults on the speed limits and people's ear drums. Maybe they let us be because we were bringing glory to Norwalk on the track. Or maybe they believed that the experienced Fusco blasting along Highway 123 at 80 mph in our hotrod was safer than the little old lady tootling along at 45 in her new Chevy Corvair. I never asked and they never offered any explanation.

It Was All Going Away...
and We Wanted One More Race.

We didn't know it for sure at the time, but I think some of us suspected it: our long summer, which lasted like twenty years, would end in a letter personally addressed to each and everyone one of us. The letters were from Uncle Sam began with the word "GREETINGS:" which really meant that you had a very short period of time to join the National Guard, the Air Force, Army, Navy, or throw the letter in the trash, pack your things and leave for somewhere like Canada (being convenient, English-speaking, and nearby).

Having had a prolonged childhood, this was a scary wake up call for all of us. One beautiful late summer Sunday in 1967 it seemed as though we all knew something was about to happen that would negatively affect all of us.

We, the Boys from B&T, had announced to friends and customers if they were not doing anything this coming Sunday, we would racing at the Dover Drag Strip, about an hour and a half from Norwalk, and there would be a convoy to the track. So early that Sunday morning our fans arrived at the B&T at much earlier hour then most had ever been there before.

We decided that the coupe should be Awakened at home one last time.

It was started up inside the garage bay and the beautiful noise resonated and vibrated every freestanding item within our building as well as inside the General Store. Just before Art, the General Store proprietor, was about to swing his door open and stand with his hands at his hips starring at the raging bull ragging full blast in the driveway, it was on the trailer and silent again. The dogs stopped barking, and all was right in the world that surrounded the B&T. Our little convoy left and headed out toward Dover with the sun in our faces and joy in our hearts. It was like going to your best friend's wedding. Everyone was smiling and happy.

By 9:30 a.m. we had arrived, and the car was inspected.

Once your race car is inspected you don't change anything. Next, we found a good parking place and checked everything: fluids, making sure the specially concocted fuel mixture was up to snuff and poured carefully into and locked away in its holding tank. Then the timing was checked.

The noise was so incredible you had to love it, or find yourself walking for a great distance to get away from the music being played out by perhaps a hundred drag cars. This was a place where the lion could legally roar. The locals who lived near the track all ran off together and would not return home for another ten hours or so. Squirrels, rabbits, birds, and a few raccoons took day trips to somewhere else.

The '37 Ford must have sensed it's future that day as Paul grinned, put the helmet on, buttoned up the seat belts, fired up the thirsty engine, and prepared to move toward the staging area.

But wait! We had all forgotten to check the air in the tires. That task was quickly attended to by everyone who had an air gauge.

It was only seconds now and Paul had the B&T car near the starting line, but would not go any further until the water temperature was where it needed to be. The same thing with the oil pressure as it rose to the proper level. When all was right inside the cockpit the car and Paul were both ready—and they knew it.

The engine revved like a bass opera singer clearing his throat. Then Paul pulled into the burn out box and was told that his rear racing slicks were wet. He gave it plenty of gas and spun the rear tires as smoke billowed out from under the fenders. The huge rear slicks which were wide, treadless, bald-looking tires that had to be warmed up so that they would grip the starting line pavement when all was ready for his first practice run.

Time stood completely still, and the noise numbed your eardrums as though there was no noise. NOTHING! Time and noise did not exist for a few fast seconds.

The fans who came along from B&T, some of whom had never been to a race or ever seen Paul and the Hot Rod move more than a few feet, were about to lose their virginity all over again.

The RPMs screamed up to 6,000-7,000 as the lights slid toward green which, of course, meant hold on to your ass because we be going full blast for a quarter of a mile.

Green light. In a nanosecond the front end of the racer surged up and forward as the tires gripped the pavement and Paul was gone. I had seen this a hundred times, so I looked around to see the reactions of our first-time friends. Wow! I could hear Lionel scream as he had done when we were shopping in the dark junk yard in Danbury when the cows came.

Others were jumping up and down, yelling, and the veterans were looking at the time clocks to see what time and speed Paul had turned.

The clocks read 12.5 / 110 mph—pretty damn good for the first run of the day. Paul was a good driver, no wasted moves, no showboating, just an honest man doing what he loved.

We had a good day, won some money, and stopped for a bite to eat and beer. Many of the first timers had such a good time they bought the beer for the B&T guys.

It was the last hurrah, as they say. Sadly.

My brother, John, received his draft notice late that Monday when his wife came flying into the station with the mail. He immediately went to see the Navy and enlisted into the Sea Bees. He believed he would like the work and, maybe, it would keep him out of the deadly rice paddies.

Once a week, it seemed, someone we knew was beneficiary of the "GREETINGS" from Uncle. It was like the toppling dominos game. Our lives changed and our long summer was over forever.

Our winter had arrived.

CHAPTER FOUR

Girls Being Girls

My recollections of Norwalk are through male eyes, of course. Cars, beer, cigarettes, golf, girls—not necessarily in that order at any given moment. Maybe quick sideways glances at schoolwork, music, or work.

So, I asked some girls (who wish to remain anonymous) and this is what they told me.

Molded by Dick Clark & TV

We were molded by the TV. The actors from the movies and series were our heroes. They molded us. They taught us what to wear, what to say, how to say it. Poodle skirts, little scarves tied around our necks, hey, are done a certain way.

It was a lifestyle thing that started about 1955 and

went very strong to the mid-sixties, when it morphed into the hippie stuff. We lost track of my generation. They were going, going, gone by that time. They either went to Vietnam, or got married and had a kid. Or both. At any rate, they were gone.

They were no longer individuals. They were just part of the masses at that time—doing the same thing their parents had done.

The wild and crazy rebel of the '50s became the housewife/mother and insurance salesman of the '60s and '70s.

But, back in the '50s in the rec rooms of the nation, the girls would watch Bandstand every day and follow the trends faithfully. The guys didn't seem to care too much about it. You'd have to use dynamite to get the guys out.

At a dance it was the guys on one side of the room, and the girls on the other side. The girls would come and drag him out once in a while, maybe for a slow song or something.

That was how it went down. Those were the rules. And we all understood and accepted.

How Dick Clark Changed America Forever

The boys liked rock 'n roll, but it was somewhere down the list after cars, girls, and getting into mischief—like stealing parts for their cars.

Our parents hated rock music. Hated it with a passion! It would, they firmly believed, turn us into lying, fornicating, despicable animals. Of course, they were partly right!

Our parents agreed that "Rock 'n Roll" was, in the words of a TV announcer, "ephemeral"— meaning short lived. Here today and gone tomorrow was a theme that many older people prayed for.

Well, that feeling was completely dispelled when "Dick Clark's American Bandstand" TV show entered our homes every afternoon for a full hour.

Clark introduced hundreds of performers that we had never seen before but knew their music. We would all meet up right after school and visit whoever had a TV and, if possible, a place to dance. We did not even bother with the guys! This was our fun (girl's fun) and even our mothers started to enjoy the commotion in the basement. At least we weren't with the boys, they reasoned, making out in the back seat of a car. They even cajoled our fathers to renovate the dark, creepy basements all over Norwalk into a finished "rec rooms," suitable even for adult guests when relatives stayed overnight.

So, it clearly was the '50s teenage girl who started the

rec-room-in-the-basement craze and totally changed the course of American society. For a few hours every day, we girls (and Dick Clark) ruled.

We all loved being together we shared our like and dislike of whoever were guests was on the show. We talked about which singer we wanted to spend the day with (later it became the night with). We taught each other how to dance—even to the slow ones.

Can you imagine today's kids walking in on the music of Elvis crooning *Love Me Tender* and seeing a bunch of girls dancing together with the lights down low? Not that's there is anything wrong with it. Although there were a couple of girls that did not like to be paired with a certain few girls, because we all thought they were enjoying it a little too much.

We learned new ways of talking in a feminine code that we could understand, but the guys were left in the dark. Once our cellars were updated into rec rooms, the arrival of beer, wine and other adult beverages was not far behind.

The renos often included a bar, thanks to our fathers' need for such accessories, because while we were doing our homework or out with the guys, our parents took over the rec room with their friends. Of course, we began taking a few sips which wouldn't be noticed and that loosened us up even more. Soon we were daring enough to tell what happened at the Drive-In or at the beach parking lot.

Not only did the music get us through the day (well, the late afternoon anyway), we also learned the ways of the guys and girls on the show; how they acted, held each other hands, the girls laying their heads on the guy's shoulder and, especially, how their bodies always seemed to be touching, and the cool clothes they wore so casually.

Pretty soon it became obvious at school who watched American Bandstand, and who didn't.

Goin' Down New York

Being a teenager in a small New England town with limited entertainment in the '50s and '60s meant that you had to be innovative and make your own entertainment with the resources available. At least some of the time that meant (a) gently breaking the rules, (b) being with guys, and (c) sex.

Breaking the rules was pretty much whenever and most of the time. Skipping school was the beginning. A few of us got adventurous once in a while and took the train to Manhattan. It wasn't that we wanted to be in the hustle and bustle, we just wanted to be anywhere other than Norwalk and it was easy to get to New York City.

Our activity list was tame. We'd walk around Times Square, grab lunch from a street vendor, stroll up Broadway looking in the store windows and pretend that we were international sophisticates. Then we hop on the subway for the squealing, rocking, terrifying ride back to Grand Central Station and home again in time for supper.

"How was school, dear?"

"Fine. The usual."

Other times we skipped school go to the beach with friends or our boyfriends. Not the public beach at Calf Pasture, but some hidden lake in the back country. Sunbathing was out (we were supposed to be in school, so a sunburn was a dead giveaway) and so was actual swimming for the girls (no swimsuits—and we weren't going in the water in our underwear during the day).

So, we'd sit around pretending we were cool, the guys would have a few beers and we would have a few sips until our teenage idols were hot to trot. Then it was like trying to fight off a deranged monkey. We soon discovered that the best way to handle the situation was to literally handle it until the cork popped.

The proud beneficiary would then jump into the (often icy cold) lake which did a "George" on him—if you've ever watched Seinfeld—and everyone went home for supper in a happy mood.

"How was school, dear?"

"Fine. The usual."

It was all just good, clean fun.

Once in a while a bunch of girls would go to the movies on no-date-Friday-night. One or two of us would buy a ticket and, once in the theater, open the exit door to let in our friends. We never got caught although I often wondered why.

The last activity (c): having sex, was usually a just-the-two-of-us activity. We weren't into group sex at all—at least not most of us—although I will relate another story in a minute.

The first sexual encounter usually took place in the cramped front seat of a car. With all of the knobs, steering wheel, and a floor shift competing for the space, we often emerging disheveled and sweaty. Then maybe we moved on to a swimming pool (although few people in Norwalk had pools), an isolated beach or, if the parents went out for an evening, a furtive and hurried bedroom session.

Guys & Girls Together

It didn't take long for us girls to realize that we couldn't live with just Dick Clark alone. We needed real, live, horny, car-crazed, beer swilling, cigarette-smoking guys to complete our lives. American Bandstand was just the warm up. The pregame show.

There were a couple of hurdles to overcome.

First of all, most of the boys had a car and the car needs gas, insurance, and repairs—so the boys had to work after school to earn money.

Most of the guys worked at grocery stores 3:00 p.m. to 9:00 pm at least two to three afternoons a week, plus most of Saturday. Others worked at gas stations, ice cream stands, or hamburger places with the arrival of Caroll's and McDonald's.

Many girls did the same. It was almost always fun, we got paid, were with the boys, and could always get a ride home. Thank goodness it was not always straight home in a matter of minutes. A scenic ride with loud rock 'n roll being pumped into our brains, or a fifteen-minute make out session, was always appreciated. No one ever went further than first or second base during the week. (With maybe a few notable exceptions.) No beer on your breath and home no later than ten.

There were several groups of girls just like the boys.

There were the smart ones with the sly smiles who thought they had everyone fooled about their extracurricular activities. But girls talk. We knew that they were all reading the same books and were not quite as timid about trying out some of their new knowledge.

Then you had the cheer leader types following the would-be stars of the football, or even the baseball or basketball teams. They all seemed willing to do anything and everything for their heroes.

We also had the music people, true rock n rollers who would sing the songs and even dance by themselves, letting everyone know they were into the music. And maybe other stuff.

Movies at the Drive-In were also a steady source of information and wonder for all of us. "Splendor in the Grass" one of the all-time teenage movies that assured us that we were not the only teens in the world suffering from terminal horniness and hormonal angst. This movie, and especially

Natalie Woods, helped make us all feel normal. Almost.

Yes, we also had our midnight swim parties, but for the most part the lights stayed off and no one was privy to watching another couple engage in anything but a kiss.

Then there were the rest of us girls. Just trying to make it through the day/night with whatever it took.

Parking with the Car Guys

Car guys had lives of their own that didn't include girls. Working during the week and then Friday nights—those were 'car nights' when the guys worked on their cars, drove their cars around, and tried to win races on the streets. Saturday nights were 'girl nights' when they worked on us, drove us around, and tried to win the submarine races at the beach.

Many of us preferred guys with cars, despite the inconveniences. Their cars gave us mobility; a way to get away from home and get away to other places like New York. Their cars also gave us a place to make out, play backseat baseball, and sometimes make it to home base. Although driving around was fun, much of the time it was just "parking."

We all had our favorite place to "park."

The beach was okay, except you could be going at it and someone would come banging on the window. "Whatcha doin'?"

Much of the time the car windows would be fogged up, but you still had to yell, "Leave us alone."

The guys knew that the Drive-In was not the place to go all the way. But a big, busy parking lot with your choice of off-in-a-corner parking seemed okay.

CHAPTER FIVE

Boys & Girls Together

Sydney & The Twins

It was years later that we found out about Sydney and The Twins. (This is where the group sex story starts.)

Very attractive teenage twin girls moved into one side of a duplex in Norwalk. That meant that another family lived on the other side of the dividing wall. That family had a son named Sydney who was a handsome, horny, teenager. And by using a bit of physical dexterity, Sydney was able to exit his bedroom window, cross the outside the back of the house, and enter the twins' open bedroom window, a three-pack of rubbers securely stashed in his jeans pocket. This started out quite innocent really. The girls from NYC knew a lot about sex but no firsthand knowledge, so they were very much interested. Sydney was just the right person to teach the basics.

First Syd decided to show the twins how safe sex could be with a rubber. "It's 99.9 percent safe," he related, unwrapping the item. "If your penis (she whispers "penis") is that freaking big, it'll never fit in me," Jany says.

Then they all laugh nervously. But the twins are getting curious.

So, Syd did the ultimate trick. He checked the hallway, went into the bathroom, filled the rubber up with water, tied off the open end, brought it back into the bedroom and tossed the clumsy monster to one of the girls.

Now remember that back then there were not many of the "thin" rubbers available. They were tough, stretchy, and thick. You could have used one as an inner tube.

Downstairs the twin's mother heard the merriment as the three tossed the water-filled rubber to each other and marveled at how well they were getting along. If only she knew how well!

Jany and Barb had a quick huddle and decided this was a good idea, but first they wanted to see his penis up close. This would be a first for them and they promised not to touch it—just look.

The room became very quiet as Syd slowly lowered his pants and, more than half aroused, displayed his wares. The twins were more than impressed.

Jany was the aggressive one and took the lead, making out with Syd while Barb went downstairs to get some sodas, and let the new couple do some pre-coupling moves.

With Barb standing guard at the door, Jany and Syd

continued their education.

Wow! Jany really liked what she was doing and what Sydney was doing to and for her. Barb wasted no time taking off her clothes when it was her turn, while Jany took the watch patrol station at the door.

This was a twice a month arrangement and all three loved it and never said a word to anyone not even their diary. Syd on the other hand was smarter and knew he had the best of all worlds. He never said a word except to let the girls know when his parents were going out for dinner and a movie— which left his home open for business.

Apparently, (you never know for sure about these "stories") the happy threesome continued on the three years, all through high school, until they set off for college. During this time neither the twins nor Sydney dated anyone else, their *manage á trois* kept everyone satisfied and happy.

A few years later, after college, the story finally broke when Jany, now divorced, returned home to Norwalk and caught her sister, Barb, in bed with Sydney.

But that wasn't the problem. The problem was that Sydney was supposedly happily married to a third and unrelated person. That really pissed Jany off. Divorced, pissed, and not having any fun, she decided to tell Norwalk's town gossip what had been going on in the duplex. Maybe she left out a few of the small details, like her involvement, but it was enough to ignite a fire storm that scorched everyone involved.

The Norwalk Drive-In

The Norwalk Drive-In Movie was an iconic cultural institution in the town. Every class and condition of human life went there, families, adults and teens. It operated year-round unless there was a winter blizzard or a torrential downpour.

I've been told of other drive-ins around the country that were dirty, with poor sound and picture quality, where few people watched the B-grade movie and cars were rocking around like crazy. One of the old teenage expressions was "If you see my car a-rocking, don't come a-knocking."

That wasn't the Norwalk Drive-In. It was spotless, clean, with quality sound and picture. They screened first run movies, During the cold weather the heaters were so efficient that you had to open the car windows. If you tried to pick it up barehanded, you risked a third-degree burn.

Of course, that didn't get in the way of fun.

The Drive-In was THE place for THE Saturday night date with a girl. Cleaned up guy, spotless car, pretty girl, a few cold ones, and all of your friends to wave to and honk at as they circled around looking for their favorite spot.

The most common problem was driving off with the speaker or heater still connected to the car. There would be a big burst of sparks dancing on the pavement and maybe a loud sizzling sound. Of course, no one stopped to admit fault; they just cruised nonchalantly out of the exit on their way to a more isolated spot for a little base running or maybe even a home run.

Most of the pranks were harmless and (don't say it!) stupid.

Like when your date went to the concession stand or rest room by themselves. Then you quickly moved your car over a few aisles (being careful to put the speaker and heater back) and wait. Your date came wandering back, then looking agitated, then pissed-off until you got out and waved her over to your new location.

"I thought we had a better view from here," you would explain. Then she would kick your ass. Or laugh at your incredible sense of humor and timing (or stupidity), whatever.

Or you might exchange cars with your buddy. When your date came back, expecting to resume where you had left off when nature or hunger called, there was you friend smiling like a fool and ruining the mood completely.

Or you might keep an eye on the rearview mirror until someone was passing behind your car. Then you both would start moaning and groaning loudly. The girl would yell, "Don't do that!" or "Stop that!" By Monday morning it was all over Norwalk High that you and Mary Lou were 'doin' it' at the Drive-In on Saturday night.

In fact, the Drive-In was the least likely place to have sex. Oh, maybe a bit of base running to second, possibly third if the couple were 'deeply in love.' But a home run? Never!

There was an admission fee for the Drive-In and once in a while guys (and their dates) would be broke. No problem! We'd cram them all into the trunk, pay admission for the cleaned up couple in the front, find an out-of-the-way space and open the trunk to release the sweating masses.

A few guys who were on the track team would jump the Drive-In fence and sprint like hell in different directions to their buddy's cars, dive in, and keep still. Few ever got caught. Either it just wasn't worth the effort for the Drive-In management to catch them, or they remembered how it was when they were kids and let it go. What the hell! They had plenty of customers who paid.

There was another pre-Drive-in ritual. Most of us would go to Vista, NY (25 miles up Rte 123) where the drinking age was 18, to pick up a six-pack of cold beer. You'd probably have one (just to test the freshness) on the way back which left (counting the sips taken by your date) four more for the movie.

Even before the cartoon it sounded like the Fourth of July as the "pop!" "pop!" of beers opening resonated across the rows of cars.

Of course, a warm summer evening, or the heater in winter, would take the edge off the frostiness, so you had to finish them before they got warm. Just to make sure everyone had a good time, Dominic (of the black Chevy Convertible and retailing cold beer in the Boys' Restroom) would cruise the rows and make a nice profit.

Chris & the Naked Nurses

One of the More Creepy Times
of My Teenage Years

Most guys will find themselves involved, more than they liked, in a more-than-creepy experience at least once during their teens. That opportunity was presented to them one lazy, crazy summer night in the late fifties.

Boys, especially teenage boys, need to work about twenty hours a day to keep their minds free of vulgar thoughts. Hormones raged overwhelmingly. You have to remember that this was an era without cell phones, portable cameras, recorders, music makers, or handheld porn. Hell, the most exciting movie that passed through Norwalk was Brigitte Bardot in a (then) very sexual 1956 movie called *And God Created Woman*. It took some guys months to get over it.

Anyway, there was this family that lived next door to the newly constructed nurse's dorm at the Norwalk Hospital. Chris was the youngest of two sons and was very active in school. He played sports, was on the honor roll, and even in a few school plays. That was during the day. After dark he became a very daring juvenile delinquent.

Four of us were invited over to his house to play some basketball. Chris said: "If you could bring along some beer, or whatever, it would be even better." Sounded like a good way to spend the evening.

We all managed to bring a little beer or wine, whatever we felt would not be missed from our fathers' stash, to the basketball court and played hard and fast for, like, an hour. We took a break as the streetlights came on.

At this time, we heard Chris's father calling out his name and of course Chris ran back to his dad and was told to keep the noise down because both he and his wife had an early appointment the following morning. So, we continued to play—quietly.

Then out of the blue Chris said: "Who wants to take a ride in my Mom's '58 Impala convertible?" We quietly jumped at the chance. Hey, who has a driver's license?

Chris looked at me. I looked at Gino. He looked at Jack and Dave. "Not me," was the only answer, but that did not stop us. We walked very quietly to the garage, opened the old wooden doors, and made sure the keys were under the floor mat. Bingo!

Time to start pushing the convertible up the street, away from the streetlight, and then gave it one big push. We all jumped into the front and back seats and coasted a few hundred feet until we heard the roar of the big V-8.

We cruised the Boston Post Road as though we were legal and waved to everyone. We later went to the Calf Pasture Beach and blew the horn whenever we saw a car parked with no lights and no heads showing. Within seconds heads were popping all over the place. It was time to leave the area as we did not want to upset anyone.

We turned back toward home. Chris then shifted

the transmission into neutral, turned the engine off, and coasted into the garage. Pretty sweet for a soon to be sixteen-year-old to navigate this big, beautiful car. We poured out of the car like Navy Seals on a clandestine mission, without a sound. We, the guests of this brazen teenager, were ready to call it a night! But Chris had one more special opportunity—to pay a visit to the pine forest along side of the nurse's dorm and take a peek.

Chris was last coming out of the garage with what looked like dark colored farmer coveralls under his arm. Little did we know that mysterious piece of clothing would serve two purposes. We would soon find out both.

We moved into the pine grove and were told to spread out, be quiet, and pick a tree with a lot of branches. We kind of knew what this was all about since there were no lights on this side of the building, no parking lot, no houses, and the walking path just a very dark area. The only lights were from the dorm rooms which, of course, faced the pine trees. Next, we played follow-the-leader, climbed the trees, and were able to find branches that would support our 120 to 140 pounds. Chris actually walked around to make sure we were in a position that would not be detected. He seemed to know at what height we would completely hidden.

So we sat, perched in the trees, waiting for some unsuspecting young woman to arrive at her room, disrobe, and walk into the bathroom, of course, in the buff.

After about a half hour, at most, we, the guests, knew

we had to get off the perch and get out of Dodge! We felt dirty, and we were more than dirty with pine sap on our hands, our clothes, and our shoes. Now we knew why our leader had this ratty old kind of jump suit to cover up his good clothes. The coveralls were a dark color to shield him from view. He had thought of everything!

It's true, boys will be creeps if given the chance, but this was a once and done deal, fini, no mas, over! Once we left the property we discussed what we had done and actually felt bad about it.

Now, don't let it be said we were nerds, because we would go for another ride in that car in a second. And we often drifted off to sleep with visions of a naked Brigitte Bardot dancing in our heads.

But this was too much, even for us.

When a guy buys a dark outfit so he won't be seen and won't mess up his clothes with pine sap in order to watch young women dress and undress, take showers, and go to bed, well, that to us, was sick.

We all realized Chris might have a problem.

In our Norwalk, Friday and Saturday were date nights. Chris stayed home (in his tree, anyway) to watch the girls get ready for their dates and the returned to his perch to see if the girls invited their dates in for some.

If you're like that, we figured you are sick, or on the way to becoming sick, and we did not want anything to do with him from that night on. I mean after all, we were mostly good Catholic boys schooled to respect women, our mothers and sisters. We might try going round the bases with Mary Lou in the back seat, but at least she was present and participating (positively or negatively) in the activity.

Within a few months of our adventure Chris disappeared, and we never saw him again. Nor did we ask why.

Fusco and Mississippi Girl

Another time Fusco and I were down in Port Chester, NY having a legal beer—our first visit to a strip club. The girls were dancing away topless in their little panties and we were enjoying it, when one of the young lovelies danced over to us. She could have had the face of a troll and her hair on fire, but our eyes were glued at her chest level.

There we sat grinning like fools when Fusco pulls up his tee, exposing his entire chest, and jumping up to do a little dance, imitating the girls. We all laughed, and the girl danced away, no doubt thinking "There's a couple of rubes!" It's truly amazing what guys do when caught in a situation where they don't know what to do.

Paul Fusco was what you would call today, "a handsome dude with great sex appeal—to the opposite sex." Me? I was just along for the ride.

Several years after graduation Fusco and I took a road trip south and ended up visiting my brother in No-Man's-Land, MS. The two of us were out having a beer in a little, old, lazy country bar on a warm, quiet August afternoon. Half a dozen good old boys were playing cards in another room, and we sat at the bar flirting and dancing a bit with two girls, one of whom was also the barmaid. She was the hospitable type, always ready with a fresh beer, which she dutifully marked down on our tab. The other, a back woodsy type with short shorts and big hair, said, "Hey, y'all got a car?"

"Yeah," I replied.

"Not you," she waved me away with her long, red fingernails. "You," the nails pointed at Fusco.

"Yeah, I got a car," Fusco finally gets it out.

"Then why don't y'all take me for a nice long ride?"

That was the end of them and my car. I was a little concerned after an hour had passed. Maybe they went for a swim, I thought. Then I thought of that movie, *Deliverance*.

Meanwhile the hospitality lady was bringing more beer. "What time do you close?" I asked.

"When you run out of money," was her sweet, smiling reply. She knew we had a ten dollar bill on deposit. After all, this was Mississippi where closing times were flexible to maximize profits.

Eventually Fusco and the bayou babe returned, clothes all askew and looking overheated. The barmaid plunked a fresh beer down in front of each of them, figuring that since the place did not have air conditioning, they needed something to cool down their ardor.

There's always a party pooper waiting to screw up the fun. In this case it was a couple of sweaty MPs who threw us up against the wall a couple of times just in case we were Uncle Sam's boys gone AWOL. They didn't think to apologize for their mistake. But the party mood was broken. The MPs were just pissed that we were having a cold one with real girls. We left the change from the ten as a tip and drove off into the humid night.

As I've said, Fusco was a handsome dude who was appealing to the opposite sex. Even though he was rather naive about the whole thing. He just kind of went along with everything with that stupid grin on his face.

Naming "The Rope"

The other afternoon after nine holes I was having a beer with a couple of the guys at the club house and we started talking about the nicknames we had in school. I was "BD" back then. My brother was "JD," so I guess we went together as a family.

That started me thinking about nicknames. Usually by the time you get to high school your nickname is married to you, a part of your being.

Take "Moose", for example—and the guy got that one because? Come on! Help me out here! That's right, he was always BIG!

Next, "Boobs." Yeah, you're right again!

Wow, doing great for both boys and girls with an equal number of assorted nicknames! Some were profane, others innocent, and could be shared with family and friends. In a few cases teachers called people by their nickname.

There is one nickname that was introduced by a girl about a guy. It came a few years after high school when girls were feeling emancipated. Cheryl was one of the nicest girls, perhaps a few years older, but special. She was proud of her sexuality, but did not flaunt it. She knew what the boys were looking for and occasionally, if she liked them, she'd share it.

Cheryl had been dating Norm for about a month

when, sitting around at Calf Pasture Beach, a small group of us were deciding what to do or where to go. Norm was walking away toward the concession stand for snack supplies when Cheryl said, "Have you ever gone swimming nude swimming with him?"

"What a question!" "Are you nuts?" "NO WAY!"

Cheryl got some push back there, but she was not intimidated. She popped a beer, fired up an L&M, and patiently waited for the noise to subside.

Once the giggles calmed, she continued. She wanted to get the answer in before Norm got back. "Well, anyway, Norm has the biggest pecker I have ever seen. It's so-o-o big you could tie a knot with it and still have enough left to do the job!"

The waves and shouts on the beach seemed really loud for about a minute, I'd guess. Meanwhile, our chins were lounging down in the sand.

Wow, that was heavy! But before anyone could say anything coherent, one voice yelled out: "I christen Norm 'THE ROPE!'"

So, at that exact moment, Norm became "Rope," or "The Rope." We had, although we didn't know it at the time, just witnessed history in the making.

Cheryl loved the nickname and as Norm approached our little cocktail party with a load of chips and hot dogs she led the chant: "We want Rope! We want Rope! We want Rope!"

Norm—I mean "Rope"—was a little embarrassed when

he found out what it meant, but he got over it in about fifteen or twenty seconds. Cheryl was smiling and appeared very pleased, obviously looking forward to a festive evening with The Rope.

What could be better than spending time on a sunny afternoon at the beach having a few beers and talking about the size of someone's private parts? Kind of sets the mood for the rest of the day, doesn't it?

A few of us used to wonder whether our parents ever talked like that or made up nicknames based on the size of a guy's man parts? Most of us couldn't ever imagine our mothers saying the things Cheryl had said. Although our fathers might have, but not when girls were within earshot.

It was also the heyday of people like Lenny Bruce who was forever getting arrested for saying "fuck" and talking about sex on stage. We all giggled. Not because he was particularly funny. It was a nervous giggle.

Like the reaction when the guy got back from summer sleepaway camp and was having Sunday dinner with his family and politely asked his grandmother to "Please pass the fucking butter." That kind of giggle.

A Goodwill Donation

You know the type of guys, white shirts, maybe even a tie, a briefcase forever at their side, and most had haircuts usually found in the Army. The girls dressed in similar modest plaid skirts and solid tops as crisp as a saltine cracker. The Nerds would always travel in a group and most times did not have a leader. Their progress into experimentation was an extremely slow journey.

It seemed for the most part the girls were more interested in what was going on with their bodies than the boys. The boys seemed to be more interested in being together and sharing a sentence or two from a *Mad Magazine*.

So teenage life then was pretty much what we have seen on TV for years. Take *Big Bang Theory* as an example. In short, the boys were clueless. Before they knew it, their high school days were gone and they still had to grow up.

College must have been a total rude awakening to them since they were so far behind in social skills. That being said, if they were really smart then they went to a high end smart factory and were at ease with an entire class of intellectuals also known as Nerds. As much as they are a necessary evil to the growth of all countries, they remain a mystery to many as to how they find a mate.

Well, right around graduation a group of Nerds showed up at Calf Pasture Beach one early June evening. They parked their cars down toward Shady Beach and were frolicking in the sand giggling all the way because they did not know what to do.

With all the noise, several regular guys who had already had three or four beers quietly went down to see what the Nerds were doing. Upon visual contact they could see a dozen or more boys and girls running around and it looked like a bottle or two of something. Too dark to tell.

Finally they could hear "Lets go swimming!" Then silence. The boys stripped to their tighty whiteys and the girls to their bras and whiteys. Off they went, not a care in their world.

But lo and behold, the watchers thought this was a perfect time to collect the Nerds clothing, both boy's and girl's. They were kind and left the wallets and car keys so they could be found. The outlaw boys ran back to their cars and drove to South Norwalk and made a donation in the Goodwill depository.

Upon a return to the beach the Nerds were gone. I'm sure they were wet and cold, and back in the day there were no cellphones, so many had to return home and explain themselves.

Sweet Mother of Pearl, what a night was had by all!

The Ballad of Anita & The Snowplow

Paul Fusco and I were attending Community College when I decided that I should hook him up with Anita.

Anita was a liberated young woman whom I dated several times. Now when you "date" Anita, it's going to be rock 'n roll in the hay all night long. My dates with her went way beyond my expectations. Also, she was not a singular girl—she enjoyed dating a variety of men.

An added note: Anita was one of the first girls to admit that she had read "The Book." "It made me a better lover," she would say with a broad wink.

It also should be noted that she enjoyed her own living quarters. Her father, a widower, lived upstairs in the family home while Anita had her own cozy, separate apartment in the basement.

One day I casually mentioned that she might enjoy Fusco's company. I also mentioned that Fusco was a virgin who was looking forward to losing said status. All he lacked was a suitable traveling companion. She volunteered without hesitation.

One condition. "You'll have to bring him to my place first in case I don't like him." No problem I assured her.

On the appointed evening we arrived at Anita's. I had a six-pack and homework. Fusco had anticipation on his face and Trojans in his pocket. Anita was plainly intrigued.

After some small talk that included Anita's father, she announced that she and Fusco were going out to get something to eat, and maybe go dancing afterward. Meanwhile, she told her father, I would be in her apartment studying.

It was obviously engrossing homework, because it was a couple of hours later when I looked up, went to the window and saw that we were in the midst of a major snowstorm. While I wondered what Fusco and Anita were doing, I was more worried about how they were doing in the blizzard.

Then I heard a car in the driveway and the two came in brushing snow off their coats and stamping their snowy boots. When Anita pulled off her hood, I couldn't help but stare at the lump over her right eye.

"Shut up and go to bed," she said sotto voice as she walked by. "I'm going to bed."

"What happened?" I demanded of Fusco. I looked out the window; no car in the driveway. "Where's your car?"

"It's a long story," he groaned wearily. "I'll tell you in the morning." With that he rolls over on the sofa and immediately starts to snore. "What a cool guy," one side of my brain thinks. "What a jerk," the other side counters. I hardly slept all night and was more than ready when Fusco woke at first light, rubbed his eyes and scratched other places, and woke up enough to tell the story.

"We went to The Hearth," he began. The Hearth was one of those local teenage hangouts in Vista, NY which accepted both fake and real IDs. You could drink legally in NY at age 18; you had to be 21 in CT.

"We had a few Seven&Sevens and danced for a few numbers. That was the warm up phase. "Then we went back to the car and, you know, did it."

I gave Paul an inquisitive look.

"I mean we did it in the front seat, the back seat, the front seat again. We melted the ice right off the windshield. Then we left."

I was impressed at his stamina.

Meanwhile the snow continued to fall rapidly, building up on the road. "I've got to get you home," Fusco decided. "I'm not stopping until I get you home." He was a single minded now-non-virgin whose mind had been poisoned by Canadian whisky and car sex.

Anita decided if she was going home in a blizzard it might take a while, so she might as well play along the way. Taking the matter literally into her own hands distracted Fusco, and perhaps he took his eyes off the road for just a second, and just at the moment of release, he hit a snowplow head on.

I sympathized. Keeping one's eyes focused at that moment was pretty much impossible.

The car, a beautiful, two-tone 1958 Impala, bounced off the plow and onto the shoulder. In a move that echoed of chivalry, Fusco grabbed Anita and pulled her from under the dash. (Of course, this all happened in the days before seat belts. Not that they would have made much difference given the activity and level of intensity.) As he straightened her up, he could already see the knot growing over her eye.

By the time the police arrived the couple had sorted themselves out, repositioned various body parts back where they belonged, and told their story, thoughtfully omitting some of the activities such as the drinking and sex.

It was the cops who had driven them home. I called my friend Fred (of the unstoppable Jeep CJ and snowplow story) who drove us over to Smitty's garage and, yes, the Impala was a total wreck. Ready to take it's place at the local junk yard and possibly become a target for midnight shoppers.

A few days later Anita's eye was a sort of vomit green color with dark purple highlights. "I can't date both of you," she announced during a stop at the B&T Texaco and left for her class at the College. So, she didn't date either of us. But that was OK with me. I was just happy that they had a good time, that Fusco was now a "real man" with all of his manly parts still intact, and that they had the unique experience of hitting a snowplow head on at the very moment of consequence and lived to tell about it.

I've often thought of awarding him a plaque that he could hang in his man cave attesting to his feat of bravery and uncommon good luck.

But instead, with all the money I make from this book, I will have a suitable plaque made and install it myself for all to see!

Swanky Frank's

No one place had a better location than this famous landmark back in the day, or night for that matter! It was right on the front row of the Boston Post Road facing all the traffic coming from the south and going to the south. There was an entrance to Route 95 right around the corner. This was one of two measured quarter mile stretches where thousands of drag races took place over the years.

Swanky Frank's was a time-honored treasure run by Eleanor and Big Al. He did all the cooking and Eleanor did everything else required to run a restaurant and keep Al happy. Neither were easy jobs, but someone had to do it and Eleanor proved she could handle it. Al and Eleanor worked a minimum of ten hours a day into night, for seven days a week from April through early November then off to Florida for some rest and relaxation.

Swanky's was pretty much a male dominated, blue-collar establishment. It had good food, was clean as a whistle, and was very reasonable. It was run with respect to the owners, plus a little fear, when it came to Big Al who was always dressed in white. Al had what the kids today might call a "resting bitch face"—not unhappy, but not smiling either. He seemed serious all the time. Then there was Eleanor, Al's wife, who managed the dining room with an iron fist in a velvet glove.

The young guys would meet there for a quick bite to

eat at any given hour of the day or night just to see what was going on. It had a counter which served fifteen people and a dining section with six to eight tables with red and white checkered tablecloths which Eleanor kept very, very clean.

So, this night four or five of us are sitting at the counter having a hot dog or a hamburger and this little foreign car comes flying into the parking lot. The dust and rocks were flying all over the place and we all turned to watch. The driver comes charging into the place and looks at us gawking at him and gets smart-ass. He gives us a second look and says, "What the Hell are you guys looking at?" His mannerisms and loud voice were meant to intimidate us. But it did just the opposite.

"Are you nuts, mister, on our turf, and in front of Al?" We looked at each other, as did Al, who gave us the eye, but not the stink eye.

The loudmouth new guy asked for the key to the restroom. Al gave him the key and we could hear the door lock click behind Mr. Smart Ass. It was pointed out by someone that we could box this guy's car in horizontally between two vertically parked cars, and the asshole would have to wait until the owner, or owners, were ready to leave the restaurant.

This we did in just a few seconds having a tackle, a fullback, a guard, a tight end, and a golfer, all lifting, laughing, and moving the car into the correct position of "no way out". As we left toward the other end of the parking lot, we could see Al looking our way and he was not pissed. Eleanor was busy in the dining room.

The guy returned from the can, hung up the key, and asked for a coffee to go. He then turned and saw his car sideways with no way out and started screaming all kinds of language. "Hey", Al said, "no more of that kind of language around here. Take your coffee, get out, and don't come back!"

It was over that fast and furious but the laughs lasted for fifty or sixty years. No one likes an asshole, especially on your own turf. Al never said a word to us just a faint little smile on his resting bitch face. We done good!

Terry & The Leftovers

Another time we were meeting at Swankys and the counter was busy. So, we went into the dining room.

Eleanor cautioned us that we could only go in there if we were going to eat.

What? Are you kidding us? Of course we were going to eat. At least those of us that had money were going to eat.

Menus were not necessary. We knew what we wanted, a Coke and a hot dog or hamburger, and maybe French fries.

There were two lovely girls sitting across from us. Terry—who had on his very best Kingston Trio madras shirt with his khaki slacks, and fresh cut flat top—started talking to them.

You know, all the small talk: "Where you from? Oh, yeah, near the? Oh yeah, I have an idea where you live in Darien. So, what are you doing up here? Going to see a friend in the hospital. Oh, okay, great stuff!"

We were impressed with our playboy hero.

Eleanor was watching this from the entrance to the dining room. She was impressed and interested.

There was one crucial piece missing in Eleanor's knowledge bank.

Terry did not have any money. And we were not going to lend him any. His past pay-back schedule was not the best, so Terry sat and entertained himself with the ladies. The rest of us were there to both eat, and to admire him.

One of the girls used her napkin and the other did the same. Which meant they were finished with their meal and they had to leave.

Terry, with a big smile on his face, asked the girls if they were finished eating.

"Yes," they confirmed.

"Then can I have your leftovers?"

Huh? What the hell, you moron! What an awful request!

I mean, if he had said: "Hey, you want to go and make out?" the girls might have laughed and said something equally bizarre.

But, CAN I HAVE YOUR LEFTOVERS? Wow! They didn't have a quick retort for that one.

The girls mumbled something, left a tip, and moved on out of the room, and the building, rather more quickly than absolutely necessary.

Eleanor, looking horrified and angry at the same time, homed in on Terry and marched him out to Al.

Since Al had not heard the original exchange, Eleanor gave him the instant replay.

The bottom line was that Terry banned from Swankys for two weeks. And if he had money, he had to show it in advance before he could not enter. Rules is rules!

Terry had to wait for us outside since he has come in someone else's car. We, or course, had to linger over our dining room meal. Terry was not happy. It was also the first time any of us ever saw someone's face turn a bright lobster red!

The Origins Of The Wave

Ask anyone. They'll tell you that "The Wave" started at some football or baseball in some major league stadium in some big city.

Well, I'm here to tell you that it started about 9:00 p.m. on a Thursday in June 1962 at 135 Patrick Ave. in Norwalk, CT, the home of our first car club.

This facility was a barn rented from Parker Dooley's dad. (Parker was one of the nerds who Mr. Duden was trying to impress back when I was sent up for detention, and so on.)

Anyway, Parker's sister was rather well-endowed and liked to listen to rock 'n roll in her second-floor bedroom with the lights on and the curtains open. That got our attention for about one minute and then it was back to the carburetor replacement.

One night I noticed that guys were leaving the barn quickly. Being the curious type, I followed. Miss Big Tease was putting on a show in the curtainless bedroom window.

As she moved to the left the boys all leaned to the left. Then she'd move to the right and the boys leaned in that direction. Back and forth she went while the group of greasy, horny car enthusiasts outside the barn raised their arms and leaned this way and that to her lead.

Truth be told, that's actually how The Wave started. It was repeated every Thursday evening throughout that summer. Not one member ever missed a meeting.

Marsha

Graduating from Norwalk High School was often a feat in itself. It meant that you had overcome the system and the staff and the studies and survive until the magical day. Then clad in your cap and gown you walked across the stage to show that you were a survivor.

Pompous speakers made serious and solemn noises about the shining future ahead for graduates as they entered the wondrous world of college, work, or whatever. They had visions of everyone becoming famous, rich and successful. They also knew it could happen if everyone played by the rules and got more than just a little lucky.

As we all know, few people play by the rules and those who do, well, success is elusive and sometimes downright cruel.

Like Marsha. She went through NHS, blonde, smart and more beautiful every year. Cheerleading, chess club, National Honor Society—you know, the girl you love to hate. Maybe a touch more daring than most of the other girls, her hair was cropped on the short side which made you look twice to ensure that she wasn't a real, live pixie.

She had earned a partial scholarship to college and, except for holidays and spring break, I didn't see her again until spring. We were at a party and she asked me if we could talk for a while—privately. We sat in my car in the dark with the engine and heater running, listening to the sounds of the party, watching people coming and going, while the story tumbled out of her between quiet sobs.

She had set off for college and almost immediately had fallen madly, passionately and hopelessly in love with this guy who, it turns out, was a real winner. He passed her around to his buddies for sex, telling her that he loved her and if she truly loved him, she'd put out. Unfortunately, she did truly love him and she did put out. When she finally saw the light, it was too late. She felt used, dirty and a failure.

"I feel that I'm walking around with a big scarlet 'A' on my chest," she said snorting onto my handkerchief.

Now she was home with her mother and father, in her old room, looking for a job.

"Why me?" I asked. "Why tell me?" I felt a bit resentful that now I had to carry around her sad tale like a heavy suitcase, but also a bit proud that she felt safe enough with me to share her story.

"You're inscrutable," she said after a long pause, her eyes locking with mine.

"What does that mean?" I knew perfectly well what it meant. It meant that I was like Charlie Chan in the movies, and no one knew what I was going to do or say next.

"You march to your own drummer," she replied taking my hand in hers and squeezing it gently. "I don't think you judge like most people. You don't think I'm a bad person just because I've done some really stupid things." Well I said this to Marsha, if you are really alive then stupidly done or conceived ideas are an inevitable. If you participate in almost any event, it's bound to happen at least once. It's part of how we learn and remember what happened to the only perfect person.

I nodded. Maybe she was right. I knew some terrible people, but I still liked them.

"Thanks for the hankie. And the ear. I've made you burn up a lot of gas tonight. Thanks." She slipped out and closed the door, gave me a little wave and went back inside. I didn't feel like partying any more, so I went over to the General Store, yakked with Art for a while, and went home.

Marsha and I became friends (absolutely no hanky-panky or bullshit—just like a guy friend) and went up to New York for a beer or to Swankys for a dog every few weeks. So, she kept me up to date on her career, which was rising.

Starting as a secretary at one of the many industrial plants in Norwalk, she soon became a planning clerk or something like that. At first the salary was menial, but with promotions came pay increases. She saved every penny with one thought in mind—get her own apartment. Within six months I was helping her move in across town. It wasn't the Ritz, but it was hers. We celebrated with beers and I spilled a little on the linoleum kitchen floor, on purpose, to baptize it. She also had matured into a very beautiful woman. Even I noticed that.

Her next goal was a car. Brand new. A convertible. She started with the cheap dealerships. But every time she walked in a showroom door she was surrounded by young, panting salesmen. She'd tell them that she was single, had a job and her own apartment. Some of the young studleys were now growing entire forests in their trousers and would have paid for the car for her if she would give them a chance.

So, she moved up in class and one winter day walked into the Oldsmobile dealership on the Boston Post Road. She saw her dream car: candy apple red, white convertible, red leather bucket seats, immaculate white walls, fancy hub caps, and lots and lots of shiny chrome.

The salesman, a middle-aged man, introduced himself, asked her to sit, got her a coffee, and asked her to describe the car she wanted. She felt comfortable at last and pointed to the red Olds twenty feet away. It took a while, but Marsha and the salesman finally worked out a deal where she could buy the car without a co-signer or guarantor.

"One more thing," she asked. "I don't want to drive it in the snow and salt on the road. Can I leave it here until the roads clear up?" The deal was made and the red Olds spent the rest of the winter in storage.

Meanwhile, things were going well at work with plenty of overtime available and Marsha was willing to work. Then, one spring evening over beers in New York, she told me that her boss had told her, in no uncertain terms, that they would have sex in the office or in a motel, and that was that. She tried to put him off and told him she was not interested. That just poured gasoline on his fire. One day after work when he got too aggressive, she pretended she was going to the ladies room, left the building and didn't come back until the next morning.

By now it was May and the candy red Olds made its appearance, much to the acclaim of her co-workers and friends. "Wow!" they said. "What did you have to do to get that car? Screw the boss?"

Well that took a bit of the shine off the paintwork. She laughed, but it bothered her. It emboldened her boss. "Everybody thinks we're doing it anyway. So, we might as well do it," was his logic.

A few evenings later Marsha and her boss were in the office, alone, finishing up a proposal. He had had a few nerve pops and his speech was a bit slurred. He had a new plan, much the same as the old plan.

He and Marsha would have regular sex and she would get a nice raise to help pay off the Olds. Then he pulled down his fly zipper to show that he really meant it.

"No fucking way. And put that thing back where it belongs and keep it there!"

There was silence for a few seconds while the boss reconsidered his offer.

"OK. Let's keep this between the two of us," he said evenly. "If you tell anyone else, you're fired." Then he delivered his ultimatum: "If you ever want another raise or a promotion, it'll take this," and he held his package in his palm.

The boss didn't know that Marsha had already made her

decision, and it didn't include what he was holding. She'd been screwed over once (literally) and it wasn't about to happen again. A couple of weeks later, while the boss was on vacation, her pay envelope contained her vacation and severance pay along with her pink slip. She'd been fired.

She called me and we had a few beers a couple of days later. "I even tried to call him at home to tell his wife that he was a bastard, but his number is unlisted, and he uses a post office box." Norwalk was not that big of a place and she could have found him if she really wanted to, but her hatred quickly ran out of steam and, now that it was summer, she decided to spend some quality time with her car and the beach.

It was a beautiful summer. Mickey and Roger and their Yankee teammates were hot. The hot dogs were juicy, and the fries were great at Overton's and the sun shone every day, and the golfers were generous with their tips. It was nearly perfect.

The white top on Marsha's car stayed down most of the summer and she cruised around Norwalk without a care. No job. No one telling what to do. What not to do. She had total control and total freedom. And she was loving it.

But she did get noticed. I mean, you have a beautiful, buxom blonde tooling around in a red Olds with the top down wearing just a little, white bikini. Even the Norwalk Police knew her routine, when she would drive to the beach, past the construction sites where the guys would wolf whistle and call out smart ass comments. Marsha would just wave merrily and smile.

Sometimes a guy would pull up beside her at a light and shout, "Hey. Do you need any help getting that suit off?" It was all good fun and, if she was offended, the big Olds engine could burn off most other cars when the green lit up.

She told me that she actually enjoyed this harmless repartee. Everybody had a good time. Nobody got hurt. And she was always in full control of the situation.

Then one day a guy pulled alongside. "Hey, Sweetheart. What would it cost to see more of you?" What the hell, she thought. Just the two of us.

"Twenty bucks," she yelled back. The guy practically bit his tongue off and gave her the thumbs up. She gave him the "Follow me" sign and pulled into the Red Coach parking lot near the Turnpike ramp. The encounter went well. Quick, clean and a return engagement was arranged for same time and place next week.

It was the first of hundreds and it went on for a couple of years. Summers in the shade and winters with the heater on. She would see her clients in Norwalk going about their lives with their wives and children, but she never made any sign of recognition. Her clients never did either. Marsha was not even jealous; she had her life and loved every minute of it, well okay most of it but like she said, "There is always an asshole? You kind of expect that in her business." It was all business, and it gave her the feeling of self-respect, freedom, and being in control. Not to mention several very healthy wads of cash rolled up in plastic wrap and taped securely inside her toilet tank. That was my idea, not original, but it made her feel more at ease. She had to get a safety deposit box and then another, business was that good.

One evening we were having a coffee and I knew something was bothering her. Hey what the hell is wrong? We were at Swanky's sitting in the restaurant side.

"I'm going away," she said sadly taking my big, greasy hands in her small smooth ones. "I love you," her eyes meeting mine. Wow, all I could think of was that she was knocked up but I did not want to ask her, she would have to tell me that.

"And we've never even screwed," I was trying to make light of a heavy situation. It was probably the wrong thing to say, but that kind of thing is what makes me famous in my little world of craziness.

Her smile turned into a laugh. "No. And we never will." Her face turned serious again. "I'm leaving Norwalk tomorrow."

"Where to?"

"I'm not sure. We're about as far east as the country goes. The Red Rocket and I are heading west. We'll stop when we find the right place."

"Will you write?"

"No."

"Phone?"

"No."

"Will I ever see you again?

"No." It was all so final. I suddenly realized that I was going to miss her.

"Thanks, Brian, for being my friend." She stood and with one last glance, walked out of my life and, as far as I knew, this part of the world. The last I saw of her were the big taillights of the Red Rocket making the turn toward the Turnpike.

"Such a nice girl." It was Eleanor, one hand on my shoulder and the other holding a wet cloth she used to wipe down the tables. "You should have married her and made lots of babies. But now, I'm guessing by what I just saw, that she's gone for good." She squeezed my shoulder a little harder and I was busily wiping my nose on the napkin and trying to rub my eyes at the same time because on some occasions I seem to get wind in my eyes.

One thing for sure where she ended up, she probably got a job and a new car, and maybe a nice house and a husband and a couple of beautiful children. She deserved to be a winner.

CHAPTER SIX

Norwalk People

The Guitar Ballad
of Link Chamberland

Lionel Chamberland was a true Norwalk legend. Type his name in your Google search box. You will be surprised to know that this man lived amongst us, and few knew it.

These days the legend is known as "Linc." Not sure where that came from, since my brother, John, and I helped to name him. We called him "Link"—as in the "Missing Link."

Lionel was a ferocious young man—John's contemporary, a couple of years older than me. No matter what he did, from a very young age, he was always driven to be the best. He was a great hard-throwing lefty baseball pitcher. If you ran a race, he was going to be first. For sure, if he was driving in a street race, you were going to lose. (Remember *The Last Race Where Both Cars Won* earlier in this book?) In music he was the very best. Even his contemporaries and competitors admitted it.

Lionel Chamberland was the only young man I ever knew that never showed fear. (Except for one instance when we were doing some midnight shopping and the cows arrived.)

If you were playing *Jeopardy* and the clue was "Cows," the answer would be "What's the only thing that Link Chamberland feared."

His first and last love was the guitar. He took lessons from the same teacher for many years as a youngster, and never missed a lesson, until the master told Linc's parents, "He now knows more than I do." Lionel went on to write and arrange music before he was sixteen years old.

In his spare time, he also found the time to fish, teach guitar, and own and drive one of the last truly fast hot rods in the area. His band, "The Orchids," regularly played from New York venues to the Country Inn, The Red Barn, and the Canada Lounge. Later they toured the US, creating a legion of fans that traveled to listen and to dance to their rock n roll music.

Part of the band and a very important part in more ways then one were the identical twins, Jim and Jack Hungaski. Both were blond, handsome, wore shades, and could really rock the sax. They had their own dedicated groupies who would descend on them to play kissy face before and after the shows

Link married Maureen Kennedy from Greenwich and had a son, Scott who followed in his father's musical footsteps. Link's end was early and tortured. He died of leukemia at age 46.

(I am so impressed with "Link's" music and story that I think my next book will be about Lionel and the Orchids and his music.)

Link's (or "Linc) as he is known there) *Wikipedia* entry ends: Tommy Mottola, who in 1990 became the Chairman and CEO of Sony Music Entertainment, called Chamberland "one of the greatest guitarist of all time." In his 2013 book, *Hit Maker*, Mottola said, "You won't find any mention of Linc when *Rolling Stone* magazine does a cover story listing their top hundred guitarists. Take it from me. In 1966, you never heard anything like Linc." Billy Vera, in his 2017 autobiography, referred to Chamberland as "the Telecaster genius."

RIP Linc.

Phil Baker

During a lifetime you meet a very few people that you can say, "They were all round the very best."

For me, Phil Baker was in that category.

His real name was Phil Matro, but he changed it to "Baker" when he started boxing professionally in and around New York. At just 5'5½", he fought 63 bouts in the feather weight division between 1930 and 1938 with a 32-27-4 record, including 12 knock outs.

He retired from the ring and moved back to Norwalk where his mother still lived and opened up an Italian restaurant with her as the cook. With Mom known as an incredible cook and Phil as a personality, the restaurant was an immediate success.

While Mom was in the kitchen, Phil was the front man. Impeccably dressed, he personally welcomed every guest and made sure they received first class treatment. One of President Trump's supporters, Roger Stone once said that he had looked everywhere, but the best pizzas he ever had was at Phil Bakers.

Growing up in Norwalk, Phil's was the only place for a special date. I might go to Uncle Joe's with the guys, but Phil Baker's was our go-to place if we wanted to impress.

Phil never forgot a customer.

One summer during the B&T days, Paul Fusco and I

were cruising through the middle of South Carolina on Route 95 when we see a car with Connecticut tags up ahead. Rolling up along beside them we realize that it's Phil Baker and some friends, probably on their way to play golf.

Phil spots us, recognizes us (a couple of no name kids in the middle of nowhere) and yells out the window, "Hey! You guys hungry?"

How can two guys our age not be hungry?

So we follow Phil's car off the next exit to a Howard Johnson's where we chow down on a big breakfast and shoot the breeze about golf and Norwalk. It was a special occasion. Like when a Shorehaven member asks the pro for a specific caddy. Makes you feel good about yourself and shows you how successful men are humble and down-to-earth while others think they are bigger than life.

Phil Baker's Restaurant has been gone for decades. It was in the way when the state was constructing the new Route 7 to Danbury. Phil passed away on November 27, 1996, aged 85 and is buried in Saint John's Cemetery in Norwalk.

He will always be one of my greatest heroes.

Lt. Colonel Henry A. Mucci

While I caddied for Colonel Mucci many times during my years at Shorehaven, it wasn't until much later that I learned why he was the "war hero' of the entire country. To a teenager like me, the Colonel was a "to-the-point" type of golfer. "How far to the green, the lake, stand of trees, or even the sand trap." He wanted the correct yardage immediately and no bullshit.

I became "the Colonel's caddy" because I learned quickly, looked after him, and there was no bullshit. In return, he made my life much more enjoyable, comfortable and affordable.

The Colonel loved routine and personal service.

Those qualities were also part of his business policy at his very successful Lincoln-Mercury dealership. He also made sure that the Shorehaven golf pro, Ralph Greenwood, had a new Mercury in his driveway every year.

When the Colonel arrived, I was always ready with a smile, handshake, and a dozen or more shag balls so he could warm up. I ensured that his clubs, stored at the pro shop, were always put away clean—and clean when he got them. When I knew he was coming I waited with the bag under the shade tree, ready to spring into action.

I would immediately place a glove, several tees, and a few ball markers in his left hand, and shake his right hand firmly, smiling and looking him squarely in the eye.

Leaving him the balls in the shag bag, I would jog out in the range, waiting for him to select a club, and take a few practice swings to loosen up before hitting a shot.

His heavy leather bag stood nearby at attention and, after a few shots with one club, he'd select a different club and repeat the routine. When he felt comfortable and ready to play, he'd wave and I'd hustle in.

He was, at least in my mind, the very model of an Army officer. Words were sparse and limited to the shot at hand. Or "Please get me a cigarette and lighter," a request which was always fulfilled post haste.

He "loaned" me to his wife, Marion Fountain, when she decided to take up golf. After countless hours on the lesson tee with pro Ralph Greenwood, she was ready to attack the course. Mrs. Mucci had a long drive, but no idea where it would end up. She teased me about getting so much exercise and getting to see a lot of places I had never seen before while tracking down her ball.

All of my caddy training, courtesy of experienced caddies like Hook and Slice, helped me handle both the Colonel and Mrs. Mucci, two very different and challenging golfers.

My training from the likes of Hook and Slice also helped me with one of the Colonels' regular guests—Ed Sullivan of the famous Sunday evening TV variety show. Sullivan was an accomplished golfer, but always in a hurry like he was being paid to be there by some sponsor and his contract was about to expire.

The first few holes were tough on Sullivan's caddy as

he chased the celebrity's hooks. My job was to stay with the Colonel and keep him from being distracted by Sullivan and his caddy looking for lost balls.

Finally, I told Sullivan's caddy to look in his bag, match the lost ball number, and hand it to him as if it was the one that went over the road and was last seen going to grandma's house.

So, the Colonel and I got along famously throughout my caddying career. It was a matter or treating everyone with respect, as the veteran caddies would say. Blend in, try to speak their language, but don't kiss ass unnecessarily. Just man up and do the job.

Years later I learned that the Colonel was a West Point graduate, a genuine war hero, and a recipient of the Distinguished Service Cross, the nation's second highest military decoration.

The Colonel's exploits involved the rescue of several hundred American POWs from the Japanese-run Cabanatuan Prison Camp in the Philippines in late January 1945. Led by Colonel Mucci, a strike force entered the camp, liberated the POWs, and conveyed them to safety. Along the way they were attacked by Japanese forces including tanks, but Mucci's forces repelled them and they made it to their destination.

In 2005 a Hollywood movie, *The Great Raid*, starring Benjamin Bratt as Colonel Mucci, was released. The Colonel, however, died in 1997.

For me, he was a fine man, a good golfer, and someone I was proud to know and serve.

Butch Gullick

You know they say that some people just grow into their careers? Well, Butch Gullick did. And early.

He grew up (the operative words here: "grew" and "up") in Norwalk and, by the time he was 16 he was six-foot seven-inches tall with the longest arms you've ever seen. Strong, with big hands, too.

So, perfect for professional basketball, you might think. Well, Butch was very practical guy and, realizing that the construction industry was booming in fast-expanding Norwalk, he quit school and became a drywall installer. Specializing in ceilings.

He could pick up a sheet of drywall, put it over his head, hold it against the ceiling joists, and nail it in place. All in one motion. No need for step-up ladders or stilts or staging. Butch was a phenomenon who always had work, even if he chose to be on the job 24/7.

He started his own drywall company and many of the new homes and rec rooms and renovations, commercial and retail, all benefited from Butch's height, strength, and experience. His was one of the fastest growing, and most profitable, companies in Norwalk.

Which allowed him to buy a car. Not a fancy ride with all of chrome and the extras, but a '57 Chevy stripped down two-door sedan. Well, it did have a couple of extras including a three-speed standard transmission, a V-8 283 cubic inch engine with a four-barrel carburetor, dual exhaust and a posi-traction 4:11 rear end.

It was fast off the line and, Butch and his brothers noted, it was even faster when the trunk was loaded with dry wall supplies. But they didn't always need their tools with them.

Then one day a surplus manhole cover mysteriously turned up. They centered it in the trunk, and it provided just enough weight to keep the rear wheels from spinning, especially when they let a few pounds of air out of the tires.

I don't know if they ever lost a race.

Even when two brothers from Darien, who liked to test Butch and his brothers, whenever they had a new speed gizmo for their beautiful twin '57 Chevy convertibles. Butch would climb into his El Cheapo model with the manhole cover secured in the trunk, fire it up, and leave them in his exhaust.

Before he was 18, Butch had it all. He married the beautiful Gina Migilioccio (Page 72 of the NHS Class of '61 Yearbook), owned a profitable drywall company, and had the fastest '57 Chevy in Norwalk.

Some of us work for years trying to figure out what to do that's right for us. Then, when we do find it, it's too late and we spend the rest of our working lives wishing we could do it.

Then there are guys like Butch and John Kurtzman who find their life career early, seize the opportunity, and do what they love forever.

John Kurtzman

John Kurtzman is part of the very fabric of Norwalk. He had a wonderful talent for lettering, free hand painting, and pinstriping cars. He used creativity, color choices, and style that no one else knew. Kurtzman often said that as a little kid he had a paint brush in his hand instead of a lollipop.

On the West Coast (aka LA, CA) cars were the main topic of conversation for almost every teenager in the fifties and well into the sixties. Several artists emerged who started pinstriping cars. John Kurtzman started doing the same and could be found on a Saturday or Sunday at Calf Pasture Beach parking lot pinstriping cars, or just simply painting a name on the side.

I can still see John jumping from side to side to make sure that both sides were the same. He could stripe your dashboard and side vent windows and they were fantastic.

I have read that John has been recognized nationally as being one of the very best and that does not surprise me. If you want a real deal on a piece of the Norwalk culture of the late fifties and most of the sixties, visit John Kurtzman at his place of creative art, 97 Taylor Avenue in Norwalk. Or just Google his name to learn more about one of the most naturally talented men ever to pick up a pinstriping brush or drive a Henry J.

Bob "Big Top" Miller

Big Top Miller, the Norwalk native who played seven seasons as left defensive tackle for the National Championship-winning Detroit Lions apparently got his name from the time he went on a tryout at the University of Virginia and had to use his old green and white Norwalk helmet because the UVA helmets were too small for his huge head.

Bob (Big Top) Miller was a late bloomer. He played for the NHS team, but spent most of his time polishing the pine because he was small, although extremely fast. In his senior year he probably weighted 175. That all changed after high school while he played minor league. He put on another 50 pounds, shot up to 6'3" and weighed in at 245 pounds. And he was still extremely fast.

As one coach said, "He was big all over!" Huge and extremely strong hands. One of his nicknames was "Rivets" because if he got hold of you, it's like his hands were riveted in place and down you went.

After the UVA tryout he was awarded a full scholarship.

The Miller family was not unlike the Reagan family on the Blue Bloods TV series—it was a family of cops. Up on Magnolia Avenue, near the hospital, was the Miller homestead. On days when the Lions games were on radio or TV there would be several police cars parked around the house as friends and relatives watched. We used to say that would be a good time to rob a store or knock over a bank because the police were all busy watching Big Top.

At one point during his UVA career, as the story goes, Big Top decided to come home to Norwalk and become a cop like his older (huge and football famous) brother, Moose. But, he was overpowered by the family and was soon, with his father at the wheel, in the car and on the way back to Charlottesville.

After playing for the Lions Big Top became a successful businessman and racehorse breeder in Detroit.

Always a proud Norwalk native, he would return home to share stories at the Laurel Athletic Club, and humbly say that he was going to be a policeman like the rest of his family, but football got in the way. Unfortunately, cancer got in the way of his long life and he died in 2009 at age 76.

If you were ever pulled over by his brother, Moose, you could always say that you were rushing home to see his famous brother on TV.

Everett Baker

At Norwalk High School we had teachers who were strange, creepy, weird and deranged, but no one like Vice Principal Everett Baker. Part of his duties included doling out detentions to students who broke the rules.

He was fair, but you could not (as they say) blow smoke up his skirt. Mr. Baker had seen and heard most of the stories and excuses that lined his office walls like bizarre wallpaper.

He was fair. If a student was late for class or fell asleep in class, Mr. Baker would try to find out why. If it was because the student had to work late to help his mother meet the rent or buy food, the penalty was not very severe.

Mr. Baker understood that each student had different needs and treated each case separately. His outward appearance was of a warden at a high security prison, and part of that was his ever-present cigar (not on school property, of course) and non-smiling face. He helped many NHS students get through high school and junior college.

John Cavanagh

John Cavanagh's family are still residents of the beautiful, old family property on Old Saugatuck Road overlooking the Shorehaven's 14th green, the wonderful par three fifteenth hole, and the surrounding natural marshland along Long Island Sound.

A life-long Democrat, Cavanagh and was once the Mayor of South Norwalk. He then followed up by becoming the Mayor of Norwalk when both South and Norwalk became one. He owned the American Hat Company which had offices and a retail store in New York.

Many in the Democratic Party wanted him to run for governor, but his business kept him extremely busy and he declined.

Here are just a handful of what Mr. Cavanagh accomplished in his lifetime. He was very instrumental in the creation of the Norwalk Hospital, The Merritt Parkway, and the Kiwanis Club. He was on the board of the State Prison committee, the Norwalk Housing Authority and, if that were not enough, he was one of the founding fathers of The Shorehaven Golf Club. All this while he and his family remained close with the Kennedy Clan from Cape Cod. He lived a very long and honorable life, and both he and his wife passed away in 1957.

His son J. Garvin Cavanagh became the president of

the Cavanagh Hat Corporation but became disenchanted with the business world. By 1961 he had become a Roman Catholic Priest trained in Rome, returning to Norwalk to spend several summer months at his beloved home. He created a stir when he resumed pursuing his lifelong passion—golf—on what could be considered his personal playground. He remained a Catholic priest until his passing at age 65 after a long illness.

Some also "complained" that Father J. Garvin was not only a good golfer, now he also had God on his side. "Just not fair!" they would moan

It has been said the JFK actually hurt the hat business because he almost never wore a hat. This was once pointed out to JFK by another Norwalker, Al Webb, who became head of the Cavanagh Hat Corporation after J. Garvin resigned. Later, during photo opps JFK, would always carry a hat with the Cavanagh label in plain sight. It was obviously a close relationship.

Jerry Fishman

Jerry Fishman was the greatest football player in the history of Norwalk.

Now that we have that established, he was also a star in basketball, track, baseball, tennis. Did I miss anything.

He was called "Raging Bull" behind his back. Never, ever to his face. If you wanted to live. He singlehandedly (literally) initiated a bitter feud between the University of Maryland and the U.S. Naval Academy that prevented them from playing each other for 40 years.

Quite a resume!

Jerry attended Norwalk High School where he became the second all-time single game rusher in the state with 342 yards in 1960.

He moved on to the University of Maryland where he played as a linebacker and tailback. In 1963 he was the team's leading rusher with 480 yards on 116 carries and was named to the ACC first team as a guard in 1964.

That was the same year he made football history.

In a hotly contested game against the U.S. Naval Academy, Fishman responded to alleged anti-Semitic taunts from Naval Academy fans by giving them the finger. Twice. Fishman refused to apologize.

It took Navy 40 years to get over it, refusing to play Maryland again until 2004.

I remember Jerry as an NHS student always moving swiftly through the halls carrying lots of books and papers. He took all of the college placement classes with the nerds and had a foot firmly planted in both the sports and nerd camps. He even socialized with the nerds at times and the nerd girls would get all flustered and giggly when he turned up.

Once I saw just how intimidating and powerful he was. Loping through the NHS halls Jerry had a head on collusion with an underclassman. Books and papers and important documents went flying everywhere. The Raging Bull calmly reached out and got a firm grip on the back of the underclassman's neck. Very quietly (I couldn't even hear exactly what Jerry said) he instructed the guy to pick up everything and return it to him. The guy did so and after several apologies, was allowed to go on his way.

Jerry sprinted off again to his destination.

The only person at NHS who had no fear of Jerry was Vice Principal Everett Baker. Mr. Baker was in charge of discipline and detentions and if he felt that the awesome and fearsome Jerry Fishman deserved a detention, he got and served his detention.

The LaJoie Family

A number of Norwalk families had roots in Quebec, Canada including the LaJoie family. When I was growing up they were in the towing, auto salvage, scrap metal and used auto parts businesses. It was in the latter business where I got to know them. My family, brother John, the guys at the B&T Texaco—we all were into old cars that frequently needed used/salvaged/repaired parts from tires to distributors.

There were two French Canadian families in the auto salvage business operating side by side—the LaJoies and the LeBlancs. Since we shopped on price (everything else being equal) we would often visit both establishments to compare before making a decision. It wouldn't surprise me if the two families phoned each other with information on who was coming, what they wanted, and how much they were willing to pay.

By the time our hot rods were in prime operating condition, they had plenty of parts from both families. Then, of course, we sold the cars back to the salvage yards when we were finished with them and the parts got recycled all over again. I often wondered how many times they would sell the same part.

The families often spoke French among themselves when negotiating with us English-only guys. That made it almost impossible for us to know what they were saying. Once, one of the guys with us was Paul Guimond. He stood listening to the back and forth in French and finally spoke up—in French: "I think the first price is better than the second." There was total silence for a couple of seconds. Then everyone was talking and laughing nervously and we were offered the lower price. The boys behind the counter hadn't realized that Paul spoke French and understood their every word.

"Couple of smart asses," was the English words we heard as the door closed behind us.

Apparently the LaJoie racing tradition started with brothers Don and Roger running old wrecks around inside the salvage yard; up and down the aisles. Don was usually the winner and he soon started racing for cash and trophies at the Danbury Speedway, establishing his number 711 as a top competitor. Over his career he won more than 60 races and, what was even more astonishing, won five Championships over six years and got himself a place in the New England Auto Racers Hall of Fame.

Don's son, Randy, was kicking butt in the Kart series and won the Busch Series Championship in 1996 and 1997. Then he moved on to NASCAR, eventually making way for his son Corey, who has been breaking records (and a few cars) for the past few years.

There was an interesting incident a few years ago when Corey traded some sheet metal and passed a car driven by Reed Sorenson during the qualifying for the Daytona 500, putting LaJoie into the field for Sunday.

Commenting afterward, Corey was quoted as saying, "If that had been my mom, I probably would spin her out, too, to make the Daytona 500."

In Norwalk they like to go fast, so don't get in the way.

Jeep Jackels

Norwalk, along with the surrounding towns like Westport, Darien, Norwalk, Silvermine, and Stamford were inhabited by an eclectic group. The super-rich, who might have one of their homes in the area; the rich, who probably commuted to their high-powered jobs in New York City; and the famous, who were often entertainers or media personalities. And then there were the rest of us.

One of the famous (and perhaps rich) was Jack Douglas (born Douglas Linley Crickard in 1908) who became famous as a comedy writer for the likes of Red Skelton, Bob Hope, Woody Allen and Johnny Carson, as well as writing a dozen best-seller comedy books. Who remembers *My Brother was an Only Child* ?

The book in which the *Jeep Jackals* is featured is titled *Shut Up And Eat Your Snowshoes!*

Jack lived in New Canaan with Reiko, his third wife, who was a singer and comedian and famous in her own right. Reiko was Japanese and had the most beautiful, long, black hair. They also had a wolf—at least it looked like a wolf—that apparently came from their days running a wilderness lodge in North Bay, Ontario, Canada.

So, now that the introductions are over, on to the story. My friend Fred, newly married and constantly broke, had an old four-wheel drive Jeep CJ5 and did a bit of snowplowing to help pay the rent. I think it was in 1966 that we had a huge blizzard—blew and snowed for a day and a half straight.

Fred was exhausted, seeing double, and hungry. He stopped at a pay phone and called me. "Been goin' for 18 hours," he said. "Can you take over for me? I still got a long list of customers to plow out. You take the money, pay me fifteen percent, and buy the gas."

"Sure," I agreed. Fred swung by my place, I took him home, and then picked up Joey; he knew every street in New Canaan and I knew most of the people on the Norwalk and Silvermine list.

Snow plowing is not exacting like brain surgery. It's more like ram, wham, lift and push. Then back up and do it again. Also, you got paid the instant you were finished. It's cash on the barrel head business.

People are funny about paying later, especially if the sun came out and did the job for them. Everyone knew the rules.

One note: Driveways in the upper snotty parts of New Canaan tended to be long and, often, winding roads. Owners tended to be overfed and disposed to heart attacks. Nor did their town cars have OEM attachments for a snowplow. Thus, the need for people like us and vehicles like ours.

After a couple of hours on the job Joey and I were feeling pretty confident. We had cash in our pockets and hadn't accidently knocked over any trees, sheds or houses yet. Next on the list was Jack Douglas.

Reiko, his wife, came out accompanied by the wolf. We

stayed safely inside the Jeep. Then Jack appears, ties the wolf up in the garage and says to us, "How much?"

"$35," was my reply. We usually charged $25, but the Douglas's had a pretty little Japanese bridge in the middle of the driveway which would require a slower brain surgery technique and less of the quicker ram/wham.

Jack complained a bit then told us to go ahead. I managed to leave the bridge intact and went to collect our fee. Both of them came out to inspect. That was unusual. Nobody ever came out in a blizzard to check to see if you left a few flakes on the concrete. Anyway, they couldn't find any problems and asked us to shovel out the walkway.

"Ah, no," we responded politely. "Takes too much time, it's not what we do, please pay us now and we'll be on our way." Probably those are not exactly the words we used.

Jack came back and handed us a check, indicating we should be on our way and not hang about. There were customers waiting. We were at the end of their driveway when Joey took a good look at the check. "It's for $25," he revealed. "Not $35."

Talk about being pissed off! We grabbed a few beers and a sandwich at a local watering hole in the center of New Canaan and discussed revenge.

With the lights and radio off we drove silently into the Douglas driveway, dropped the plow and filled their driveway, up to the bridge, with a six-foot-high wall of well packed snow. Then we quietly left, and continued on to plow out other happy customers, several of whom rewarded us with coffee, hot chocolate and a few shots of belly-warming brandy.

The next day, naturally, Jack Douglas called Fred (the Jeep owner) and voiced his displeasure. Fred was not really upset, because Jack only called on him when he couldn't get his regular guy. He went over, plowed out our handiwork, and announced that we owed him several beers and a full explanation—which we were more than happy to do.

That might have been the end of the story, but we found out a few weeks later that Jack and Reiko were scheduled to be guests on the Johnny Carson Show and that Jack's new book would be the topic. Carson was the best of the best and we watched regularly. Along with the wooden Ed Mahon ("Ha! Ha! That. Was. A. Good. One. Johnny.") he had a long and regular string of celebrity guests, and the Douglas's were included. The fact that Jack was one of Carson's writers probably didn't hurt, either.

Fred was a reader, when he wasn't plowing snow, and he got a copy of Jack's hot new book, *Shut Up and Eat Your Snowshoes.* "Hey guys, wait 'til you read the chapter called *The Jeep Jackals.*

The night of Douglas' appearance on Carson we got together with a few beers at Fred's place. Johnny wasted no time before asking about the Jeep Jackals. Reiko got very excited and went off on a hilarious, animated monologue on snow plowing and what happened that night. We were completely in awe, slapping each other on the shoulders and back, clinking our beers, and jumping around; they were talking about us to millions of viewers on national TV.

I have to give Jack Douglas a lot of credit. He was no doubt pissed off at the time. You head out your driveway to go to an important meeting in New York and find that your freshly plowed driveway is now impassable because you shorted the plow operator out of ten bucks. But he made it into a story that helped make him a lot of money and unwittingly treated three guys in Norwalk to an evening of TV they'll never forget.

Oh, and Fred never asked Joey and I to help him with the snowplowing again. Wonder why?

CHAPTER SEVEN

Life & Death By Two Iron

Who was it? Lee Trevino? Well, some famous golfer once (allegedly) said something like, "If you're caught in a lightning storm on the golf course. raise a two iron over your head." Asked 'Why?' he responded "Not even the Almighty can hit a two iron."

Golf is an ancient game. It is believed that "modern" golf originated somewhere in the 1600s in Scotland. Scots are, as everyone knows, a perverse lot who enjoy fighting, haggis, malt whisky, golf, and wearing brightly patterned skirts. Oh yes, they also have an affinity for a so-called musical instrument that is diabolically difficult to play and sounds like someone slowly squeezing a house cat to death.

So, in a nutshell, Scots like the challenging, arcane and weird. We Irish, for some unknown reason, like to emulate them in certain ways: Irish bagpipes, Irish whiskey (notice the additional "e"), fighting (of course), and games that emulate golf. But we did, with all good sense, move to our own large island some centuries before golf.

Growing up in Norwalk, at some distance from my Irish roots, the golf gene in my DNA stretched itself and took over. For most of my life, so far.

Some people learn many different things right at home. Others need a more formal setting, like school. But many young boys, back in the day, were lucky enough to learn more than some people ever learn in just a short period of time.

I can truthfully say that everything useful that I know I learned at the Cathedral of Learning—the caddy yard at Norwalk's Shorehaven Country Club. Well, almost everything.

My father, an avid golfer, taught me how to properly grip the club, swing back, hold it, and swing through. Then he encouraged me, and many other guys in the neighborhood, to caddy at Shorehaven.

So, by the time I showed up green and trembling at the caddy yard, I already knew how to play golf. The learning I'm talking about covered just about everything else in the world.

Celebrated as one of the most beautiful courses on the East Coast, the Shorehaven fairways and greens overlooked Long Island Sound. Designed by Willie Park, Jr and Robert White, it's a 6,500-yard challenge.

The renovations in the recent past changed Shorehaven back to more of a links type of course from its original configuration. The "links" dates back to the origins of the game in Scotland with flatter fairways and bigger greens.

The huge trees that lined many of the tight fairways were removed which allowed the grassy areas to flourish. The course now has spectacular views over the Sound from almost anywhere.

The modern (aka younger) player can use their hi-tech equipment and play a long ball game without the fear of landing behind a mature tree. The downside is a rough that is more lush, a penalty meant to be a trade off for those long drives gone astray.

The membership of Shorehaven (when I caddied there) was a wide cross section of humanity—the good, the bad, the ugly, and the miserable cheats. Yes, golf is a game that lends itself to massive cheating. Forget a stroke or two? Who's counting? Hook into the woods? Oh look! My ball must have bounced off a tree and landed right here in the middle of the fairway. How convenient. The caddy sees all. But, depending on circumstances, may not tell all. And that can lead to a very nice tip at the end of the day.

Ralph Greenwood

For 37 years the dean of the Shorehaven Cathedral of Learning and Golf Club was our beloved golf professional Ralph Greenwood. In the world of golf there are perhaps three different kinds of professionals.

One is the Professional Golfer who is primarily a player of great ability who earns his living by playing tournaments, aka The PGA Tour. Next is the Teaching Professional who may work at a private or public facility, or even a driving range or indoor location. His life's work is to promote the game by teaching beginners, as well as helping experienced golfers lose that bad move in their swing.

The last category of Golf Professional is that dedicated person schooled in all areas of being an accountant, a teacher, an organizer of member events, a presenter of awards, and an enthusiastic mentor of the entire membership. Plus having a game decent enough that only requires a few swings, and maybe a half a dozen practice balls, and the golf pro is ready to shoot anywhere from under par to a few over at any time. This is fair warning—don't challenge your home pro because he will beat you every day.

Greenwood was our home pro, the fastest talking man I ever met; he talked faster than my ears could hear. He also smoked anything that could be lit. Of course, back in the mid-fifties almost everyone smoked something. Greenwood's favorite smoke became a long cigar that stayed firmly clamped between his teeth throughout the day.

He was beloved by members and staff alike as a pro's "pro."

Caddying

You have to remember there were no golf carts at this time. They didn't become popular until later in the '60s.

So, there were on any given play day at Shorehaven during the season, between forty and sixty pre-teen boys, teenagers, and a few adult men waiting to caddy for the members. Most were part time summer kids, trying to make a fast buck for a weekend date or to buy a few beers and some gas.

Having your own money (allowances were rare in those days) led to more freedom. Some were college kids making money, working hard, and saving for the fall term.

There were a few life-long caddies, like Hook and Slice, brothers who helped educate the newbies. They would school us on how, and (more importantly) when, to talk to a member, and how he or she was your employer for the day.

All of this learning, they stressed, would make you a better person and a great caddy. And more than likely, you would earn a larger tip at the end of the loop. For me, it was more fun learning from true experience than from a book. Of course, some of the language used could not be put in a family-style book, especially if you screwed up and the teacher, Hook or his brother, took it upon themselves to correct you.

Hook and Slice (legendary caddies at Shorehaven) were

brothers, Black, in their late 30/early 40's, well over six feet tall, and looking like they could have been basketball players a couple of decades and a few thousand beers ago. They had been Shorehaven caddies for a good 20-25 years when I was there.

Neither one of them owned a car, so they arrived by bus bright and early. Many of the bus drivers let them off at a ghost stop nearer to the Club than the regular stop, but no one complained. The caddie yard was still a good mile away up a pretty steep hill. Of course, that didn't matter to the members. You wouldn't see any of them taking the bus to play golf!

The brothers were tough, strong, and capable. They hiked a mile from the bus stop to the caddy yard, then another four or five miles for 18 holes carrying two bags, then back to the bus to go home.

Some of the caddies really gloried in their strength. They'd straight arm hoist a bag on each side, holding them by the straps, and carry them along without putting them on their shoulder. By the time you went home, you'd worked a full day and loved every minute of it because it was never work. Just think: Walking around for four hours watching others play a game that you enjoyed, listening to for (the most part) pleasant conversations and being financially rewarded at the end of the round. Being out in the fresh sea air was invigorating and created an enormous appetite.

Caddying was a cash-only position, which could, in the

right circumstances, lead to some abuses. It was rumored that some of the caddies (and the names "Hook" and "Slice" may have been included in these quiet conversations) were 'on the dole'—drawing welfare or unemployment insurance—while making cash bucks at Shorehaven.

I'm sure that the members couldn't be bothered asking such questions. And they certainly weren't going to be handing out 1099-A's for their fees and tips. Besides, they were skilled teachers and deserved to be paid for their life-long lessons that they were willing to share with the newbies.

Golf was a summer-only sport, too, and people needed an income during the rest of the year. So, who minded a little extra during the summer. Being big guys, Hook and Slice could easily carry two bags each and double up the money.

The caddy yard was an ethnic melting pot and a good example of puberty on steroids. One of Greenwood's chief goals was to maintain control and complete authority, without raising his voice, while taking a casual morning stroll through the caddy yard.

It was like being in Little Italy as well over half of the caddies were Italian. That meant we got to learn, without books, many a new word or phrase, all of which had great meaning. Of which you couldn't repeat at home or school, but it worked pretty well around the neighborhood with the non-caddies.

One of the really cool things was that if Ralph came

out in front of the caddies and yelled out "Gino," half a dozen Ginos would step forward. There was Gino Vitale, Gino Di Argentini, Gino DeMarco, and a few others. Now if he were to say "Tony" or "Joey," half the caddies would step forward. Having a name like Hook, Slice, Chico, Shank, Jack, Marvin—or even Brian—helped a caddy to gain passage to the moneymaking side of the yard.

There was an etiquette to be strictly observed with Pro Greenwood.

Nodding and saying, "Good morning, Pro," got you a glance of recognition and a silent ranking on the roster of caddies who would be chosen to work that day. Running ahead and picking up a scrap of litter, and expecting recognition, got you nothing. The Pro didn't like ass kissers.

What I guess he wanted, and received often, was a level of respect when he walked through the morning throngs of caddies. While pros today wear what I would call "golf gear," Greenwood often wore a suit or a sharp, but conservative, sport jacket and tie, with a brief case in his hand.

What everyone learned quickly was this: If you got on the wrong side of Greenwood, or one of his assistants, your likelihood of caddying that day was slim, very slim.

Ralph ranked his caddies by desire, need and ability. Displaying those attributes was how you climbed the caddy yard totem pole, which led to getting better players— and better payers. Many of us considered a class in basic psychology, albeit of the street variety. Once you were rewarded by your efforts you never forgot the lesson.

That meant that experienced caddies like Hook and Slice, who turned up bright-eyed and early every day, and obviously needed the money, got the best players, payers and tippers. Caddies like me, who weren't dependent on the job for rent and groceries, had to make up the shortage with extra desire and ability. I worked hard on both, and after my first year, Ralph realized I was there for the love of the game! He was one hundred percent correct.

Being a golf pro was a tough, but lucrative, job. The Club built a pro shop, which they then turned over to the pro. The pro stocked it with golf gear and merchandise, which he sold at a handsome profit (with the Club's blessing). Members stored their clubs at the pro shop at about $40 a year when I was a caddy. Take 200 members and do the math. He also taught—maybe 500 lessons a year at $30. That was the pro's money. Plus, he received an annual salary from the Club; maybe a bonus if everything went well.

And Shorehaven loved Greenwood. Golfers want to go with a winner (who doesn't?) and having Ralph Greenwood as the pro enhanced the reputation of the Club, helped bring in new members, and was a benefit for everyone.

Greenwood worked hard for every nickel he earned. Every morning between 7:30 and 8:00 a.m. his wife dropped him off at the Club; always in a new Mercury thanks to Colonel Mucci's dealership. (Shorehaven members looked after their own!) Mrs. Greenwood would be back in the new Mercury around 6:00 p.m. to pick him up again.

Eleven hours a day at least six days a week.

One of the perks of being a high-profile golf pro was having your name on the clubs sold in your own pro shop. The owners of the Pedersen Golf Club Company had a corporate membership at Shorehaven and made most of the clubs sold at the club. There was "Ralph Greenwood" on the back of the club head. That, in itself, added a little more class to your new set of clubs.

Being a successful golf pro involved being in several places at the same time. Club members expected the pro to be around the shop to talk and recommend, and just be available whenever they wanted him. The members also wanted their pro to be a high-ranking player at the Monday pro and pro-am tournaments. That meant he had to practice every day on the driving range and putting green, as well as actually playing the course constantly.

Of course, this all required 48-hour days. Ralph had to make a choice. Although he was an excellent player, he chose to be a golf teacher, run the pro shop and the caddy yard, and stay with his family on his only day off. He had already played in a lot of club pro events in his early days of being golf professional and won a few.

Down Time

Golf wasn't the only game being played around Shorehaven. While the members might be having a "friendly game" inside over good Scotch and cigars, outside there were fun and games, too.

Put a combination of a yard full of teenagers, nothing to do but wait, and warm weather, and there will be activity.

When we were hanging around in the caddy yard— and there was a lot of that if the day was overcast or threatening, we'd play "roof tennis."

Roof tennis was a combination of handball and something of our own invention. First, you need a building with a fairly steep roof and no gutters. The Shorehaven pro shop roof was ideal. The object was to hit a tennis ball with your hand onto the roof and have it bounce at least once before rolling back down. Your opponent would have to hit the ball back onto the roof, and so on.

If you had perfect timing and could jump high enough, you could hit the ball at the right time to smack it back onto the roof before your opponent had time to react. With a couple of good players working up to 21 points, the game could go on for as much as a half hour or more.

If one of the players was tagged to caddy before the game was over, the one with the most points at that moment won. Or the game could be continued later. I remember one roof tennis expert aptly named Robert E Lee, one of the youngest but one of the best.

On occasion money would change hands, which was a bonus.

Other games were played for money such as Black Jack, Gin Rummy, Poker, and a great little Italian card game called Brish, which could be played one player against another or teams of two against each other.

Dice showed up but were discouraged by the entire staff of the pro shop. Too "street level" or "gangsterish," I think.

Irish poker was played using dollar bills with a winner take all could be very rewarding in a single hand depending how many were in each hand. If there were five players and you won you got everyone's dollar. If you had a limited memory it was best you did not participate in this game.

Ladies Day

Tuesday morning was ladies' day, and around 8:30 a.m. all the women that were playing would burst out of the ladies' locker room. Ralph would mumble through his cigar: "The locusts are coming," and quickly get out of their way.

It seemed like a hundred ladies came at us all at once in the Pro Shop, but in truth, it was more like thirty to thirty-five. They would admire and touch all the new items in the shop, running back and forth, chattering away to each other. They were like an unruly Girl Scout troop at Christmas unwrapping presents and making a mess.

They were always in a hurry and soon, like a flock of birds, left the building as one. To give them their due, later in the week many of them would come in to buy something that they saw on Tuesday—and say, "Thank you."

Ralph had caught on to this potential Tuesday riot in the Pro Shop and preferred to be "very busy" somewhere else. Around 8:15 Ralph had a regular caddy lesson. He would grab a caddy or two and give an impromptu lesson while the other caddies chased golf balls.

This served two important purposes. It kept Greenwood out of harm's way with the ladies, and the caddies got a free lesson.

Some sessions lasted longer than others because, between the speed of Ralph's speech and the ever-present cigar, he had to repeat himself several times. He was an excellent teacher, and many caddies would volunteer to shag balls or be the student.

His style was very similar to that of Ben Hogan: A controlled back swing with a full turn, a slight pause, a full body release through the ball, and hold or stick your finish. He also wanted his students to 'stay smooth.'

Getting Paid

The pay for caddying was OK—for the 1950s. Remember, gallon of gas was about twenty-five cents; a pack of smokes in the twenty-cent range; and a can of beer maybe fifteen cents.

Caddies were divided into three categories: A, B, and C depending on experience, ability, and how we interacted with the members. "C" caddies got $2.50 per round plus tip; "B's" got $3 plus tip; and A's went up to $3.50 plus tip.

Depending on the generosity of the member, number of bags you carried, the weather, and the mood of the golf gods, tips could range from fifty cents to $20. "C" caddies could expect the member to round up their $2.50 to $3; "Bs" and "As" might get an extra buck or two.

However, remember I said that the tip was up to the member. Some always tipped well; some were more frugal. Then you had The Cheater.

Caddies who actively facilitated, or simply overlooked such goings on, might get $5 or even $10, especially if there were bets on the play. A caddy carrying two bags for two cheaters could strike gold and walk away with $25 or more for the day.

Norwalk and Shorehaven produced a number of world class golfers, not the least of which was Jerry Courville Jr. who was prominent during the mid-1990s. Jerry Jr. was also a Shorehaven member, on two Walker Cup teams, had the most match play wins in US Mid Amateur history, and won the Met Golf Award 2002 Player of the Year. The trophy he took home had been named for this late father who died of cancer in 1996.

Courville was the best we had, and members had bragging rights for close to 40 years. Next came Mike Vitti who partnered with Jerry to win team competitions in Better Ball events like the Ike in New York and a few others.

Shorehaven was also famous back then for its natural

saltwater swimming pool located right on Long Island Sound. The floodgates were opened on the incoming tides so the pool would refill with "fresh" seawater.

Fire at the Clubhouse

As at most courses, the club house was the second most important place. At Shorehaven the facility was modern, circa 1950ish, well-equipped and faced the 10th tee along the back nine. There was the required (bragging) bar, dining room, trophy cases, and all of the golf memorabilia and tchotchkes hanging on walls and covering every flat surface.

It was one of the top venues in the City for weddings, parties and other tony events. Then, on Monday, October 7, 1957 fire destroyed the facility. The good news was that the club house was separate from the pro shop where the members stored their clubs, so the game was still on.

Not to be outdone by a mere fire, the staff quickly set up a couple of portable johns and a big circus tent with tables and a bar. My neighbor, Grace Rizzo, installed a jury-rigged kitchen to cook up meatball grinders and her famous pizza. She was also very generous and, being a growing boy, I never had a hungry moment that summer. Grace's famous pizza was pan fried in just a little olive oil so it would rise up and be extremely light. Then Italian "gravy" (that's what non-Italians would call "sauce') on top with mushrooms and different cheeses. Yum!

Since the pizzas were such a hit, Grace expanded her offerings into meat ball, sausage and peppers sandwiches. That required a fridge and of course that needed electricity, so Grace ended up with a working kitchen much to the delight of the members.

When the new club house was completed, she moved her operation to the pool where kids would scarf down a pizza and jump right back into the water. Some mothers were less than happy with that, back in the era where you were supposed to wait for two hours after eating, lest you develop fatal cramps and drown.

After the clean up and excitement about the fire, Shorehaven life settled into the new style. Golf for both the ladies and men continued, albeit the 19th hole was somewhat lacking. Events went on, winners were celebrated and plans for the new club house were circulated. Men drank their beer outside and looked for shade. Card games and darts were on hold unless the weather was cool.

In fact, Shorehaven was slowly settling into a very boring routine.

The Great Shorehaven Football Game

Then, one hot, humid afternoon, as the members, staff and caddies were sitting around sweating, a football flew through the air and caught everyone's attention. Suddenly guys were up and began throwing the ball around on the freshly-mowed grass behind the ninth green.

"Great stuff!" I thought. Here were a couple of dozen men, whom I thought could only walk and swing a golf club, running around hooting and hollering, throwing and catching a football like kids.

It wasn't too long before some of the older and bigger caddies were drawn into this once-in-a-lifetime spectacle. At that point some of the older members retired early for another beverage and get a good seat for what they knew was about to happen.

"Let's have a game," someone shouted out, pouring high octane gasoline on a raging fire. "Members against the caddies."

I knew in my heart that this was not going to end well. I mean, a bunch of stalwart members, pillars of the community, were certainly not going to let a bunch of snot-nosed punks kick their butts.

The caddies, of course, harbored some deep-seated resentments; cheap tippers, cheaters, mean ass players. This was their chance to wreak revenge without appearing to be vengeful.

Rules were decided (semi-touch), goals positioned, out of bounds lines established.

The game got off to a good start—for about the first ten minutes.

Players ranged from five-eight to six-two, 160 to 220 pounds. The caddies had speed and youth. The members were bigger and they could hit hard. The possessions seesawed back and forth, but the tone of the game was changing. You could tell from the sotto voce remarks on both sides.

The caddie discovered their secret weapon: Most of them spoke Italian. Calls came in two languages, but the members held their own. Scores mounted until—

From the backfield member's end came a blood curdling scream of pain. Everyone stopped. The field looked like a color photo. Nothing moved. Not a sound except the screaming.

There was Ted Gallagher, a member, on the ground, the football lying beside him, face contorted, telling the full story that something serious was wrong.

His right leg, we found out later, had been broken. The first, last, and only Annual Shorehaven Bowl was over. And winter was on its way.

After that there was a physical and cultural distance between the caddies and members that everyone could see and feel, but no one talked about. Well, maybe the caddies and members among themselves, but I don't know of any members and caddies discussing it together. It was just one of those things that no one ever mentions again. Like how come Mr. and Mrs. Turner were married in November and their son was born in late April? Like nobody could do the math?

Just as no one knew, or admitted that they knew, who had hit Mr. Gallagher. Or from what direction. Maybe he'd simply slipped and fallen down of his own accord. But I doubt that.

During the winter the new club house was being built. It was a mild winter and by mid June much of the Shorehaven life carried on. Greenwood's cigar was ever-present. Hook and Slice taught the newbies. I went on learning life lessons. The new club house was, I guess, a Colonial design with the Men's Grill kind of hanging off the back side of the building facing the 18th green. It made a great place for the members to have a drink and hoot and, in some cases, holler at their golfing buddies.

Mr. Gallagher came back to play the following year sporting a very distinctive limp, which he carried for the rest of his life, along with his signature cane.

Course Characters

Of course, we had our regular "course characters."

One couple from New York came up to Shorehaven most weekends to play: Mr. and Mrs. Max Geffen. He was a dour, grumpy millionaire who did not mind "finding" his ball in a better lie than one might imagine. His younger wife was bright, well-dressed in the latest golf attire, and played strictly by the rules—shooting in the mid-70s.

My job included having sudden eyesight problems around the husband. In other words, not seeing Max remove his ball from an unwanted spot in the deep rough, and making sure the wife was handed the correct club, ensured a $20 tip and a good day was had by all.

The Clash of the Titans

In almost every human endeavor or enterprise, there eventually comes the big showdown. That determines a loser and a winner. Coke vs. Pepsi. Mohammed Ali vs Sonny Liston. The USSR vs the US.

Sometimes the winner and the loser meet again, and the outcome is reversed. Sometimes the verdict remains for all time.

In 1960, at the Shorehaven Golf Club, history was made, and a battle decided, legends and myths were created, and two men came away: No loser and one winner.

I say "no loser" because most men at the Club were God-fearing and had total respect for Porky Manero's golf game—if not his other traits. One loss does not end a career. "Just wait until next year," has been the rallying cry for the past few decades in Boston.

1. The contestants

Porky Manero was a big guy. Everyone called him "Porky" at his request. As caddies we certainly didn't. He was also the Real Deal, The Keeper of the Coins, The Man, The Sheriff. At Shorehaven, Marero was the man to beat month after month, year after year.

His family was respected for the renowned Manero's

Steak Houses and their famous salad dressing. The name Manero's was legendary from Boston to Miami with a few stops in between.

As his name implied, he was a big guy—short, heavy, flamboyant. You might think that in late December he could grow a white beard and be delivering gifts to good boys and girls. His ride was a "Mary Kay" pink Cadillac convertible which he drove slowly up the street to the club house, much to the excitement of the caddies.

Young caddies would chase down the pink behemoth, vying to carry his clubs to the rack—and get a tip. The Pro Shop would go all a buzz. Caddies tried guessing who Manero would be playing. There was movement everywhere. It was Show Time!

Porky only played golf for money—no trophies or a dozen pink balls crap. Summer rules only (winter rules were for wimps). He played quietly, played the course, one shot at a time, never getting ahead of himself. He never three-putted. Ever. When he did speak, which was seldom, it was difficult to understand him because of the long, fat Cuban cigar stuck halfway down his throat.

We all knew Porky's routine.

First, he went to the Pro shop to pay his respects to Ralph Greenwood and catch up on the local golf gossip. "Cut the greens today?" he might ask. "Been watering a lot?" "Got any new sand out there?" "How're they rolling?" Porky knew everything about the course before picking up a club.

Then out to the range with some shag balls and a sleeve of new ones. Like a race horse, Porky never went to the tee until he was fully warmed up. On the putting green he had two putters and the results there would determine which putter would end up in the front seat of the Caddy.

He teed up high and had a short, quick swing with a good follow through.

He was, in his own way, a sportsman. Down a few strokes? Porky would give you a chance to make it up, but it would cost you a visit into your wallet to do so. Players seldom thought about besting Porky; they thought about how slim their loss would be. Then they bragged about it.

Speaking of wallets, Porky didn't have one. He did have a big roll of money, the size of a fist, in his pocket. The outside of the roll might be decorated with a twenty, but who knew what was inside. If that wad got in the way of his comfort, he'd hand it to his caddy for safekeeping.

If you haven't figured it out already, Porky was a superb golfer, but he also used outright intimidation to keep his opponents on edge.

Passing the roll of money to the caddy was just the beginning.

There was the water trick. Porky would take a big drink of water, gargle for a bit to catch the enemy's attention, and then noisily spew it out. Which everyone else consider throwing up.

Then there was the worst/best: The cigar trick.

Poked into his mouth, the big stogie was wet and chewed

and dripping on one end, burning and hot on the other. On a really important shot Porky would stand over the ball until he had the full attention of his competitor. Then he would take that slobbered-over, foul-smelling thing out of his mouth, hand it nonchalantly to the caddie (who dreading what was coming, stood rock still holding the smoldering mess gingerly between thumb and forefinger) while Porky calmly made his shot, retrieved his cigar, and moved on as if he was the King of Sheba.

Porky played as if he owned the course. Par was never good enough. If your ball was off in the bushes, that was your problem, and he certainly wasn't going to help you find it.

Putting was his strong suit; never a three-putt. His opponents would bang that birdie putt three or four feet past the pin and miss the comeback.

While Porky could be difficult and intimidating on the course, he was generous to the caddies and staff. Good tips and if you were hitching a ride home, that pink Caddy would stop and you'd go home in style with the wind in your hair and, maybe, a few cigar ashes as well.

2. The Contestants

Jerry Courville (who would eventually become the father of the famous Jerry Courville, Jr.) was a young, skinny salesman for the Pedersen Golf Company. They made the "Ralph Greenwood" signature clubs. He usually came late in the day and carried his own bag. (Remember, in those days there were no golf carts, so "carrying" was the only way to go.) Then one Saturday afternoon Ralph called for me to go grab the bag from this guy who was walking up from the parking lot.

"Son," Jerry said, "I don't have a lot of money, but I sure would like a caddy." I figured that if Ralph wanted me to caddy for him, there must be a reason. And that was how I met Jerry Courville before he became JERRY COURVILLE!

He got a bag of range balls and I started shagging for him. Even though I was moving around, he was hitting me with almost every shot. I began to pay more attention. Ralph came out, trying to make Jerry feel more comfortable. The Gang took notice, sensing blood in the water. Here was a new player—fresh money. Of course, Jerry took on them all and his wallet benefited and he went on to great heights, won numerous tournaments, and perfected his style.

That first day I noticed Jerry's style—sort of Arnold Palmer knees bent toward each other, a short back swing and similar follow through. No hook! Like Ben Hogan, Jack Nicholas, Arnold Palmer and Lee Trevino, Jerry didn't release his hands fully at impact, which helped prevent the ball from hooking out of bounds or into the high grass. As Trevino once said, "You can talk to a fade, but not a hook. A hook will not listen."

Just like in the Old West, eventually the fastest guns had to meet up on the dusty Main Street of Tombstone, at the stroke of noon, to see who was "really" the fastest.

3. Game On

I'm not sure who set up the game, although I suspect that it was Porky, anxious to show the "youngster" how the game was played and maintain his own supremacy as the Shorehaven Top Gun.

The challengers agreed to play in the afternoon, when everything had dried off. Tee off at 1:00 p.m. saw a beautiful summer day, temperature in the low 70s, blue sky with a few fluffy clouds, almost no wind. A perfect day for golf. Porky and Jerry were warmed up and ready to go.

Having caddied for both of them I knew exactly what to expect. That day I had Jerry—a special thanks to Ralph Greenwood.

The match started off with each player testing the other. A birdie here, a bunch of pars, and a few putts were conceded along the way. On the 8th and 9th holes Jerry out drove Porky by a good 15 to 30 yards for the first time that day. Both holes had wider landing areas. By the time they got to the 15th the match was even Porky had run through his bag of tricks, giving his roll of cash to the caddy for safe keeping after squirming around and being uncomfortable. He had gargled and noisily spewed water several times. Did the cigar trick twice.

Jerry played with all of the disinterest of a cloistered monk in a silent order. When Porky was doing his tricks,

Jerry took a sudden interest in a bird in a tree or a flower growing in the rough. The only times he watched was when Porky was putting, and then he watched only the roll and line of the ball.

4. The Porky Press

The 15th hole is a great par three—150 to 160 yards when the pin is on the upper level—with well-designed traps in front. Out of bounds to the left and unplayable marsh to the right and short of the green. Over the green is very bad. A week previous a member hit over the green. The caddy found the ball, but it was a day later before they found the member at someone's front door just over the border in Westport. True story; read it on the internet.

Tension was an uninvited guest as we approached the 16th tee. The everyday bouquet of low tide marshland was replaced with an air of suspense as to who would ultimately triumph.

Then Porky introduced the patented Porky Press.

Each of the next three holes would be played as a separate match. If they tied the first hole, then they played the next as a separate match, and so on.

It's been over 60 years since that fateful day, but I think it went like this: $10 on the first hole, $20 on the next, and $30 on the final hole. $60 total—real money then. And each player could increase the bet again after each hole, so the total could grow fast.

Jerry looked at Porky with an ever-so-slight smile. "Flip the coin," Jerry said,and a brand new shiny quarter that had never been in anybody's pocket but Porky's was flipped. It hung motionless in the air for a split second and tumbled to the grass. Porky won the toss. After all, it was his quarter.

The Big Man wasted no time, pulled his driver and hit his usual shot—center of the fairway short of the hilltop.

While Porky was preparing to hit his tee shot, I pointed out to Jerry that a slight wind was coming from the west, going toward the 17th—very important to know when playing the 16th.

Jerry walked over casually, teed his ball up higher than usual, looked over at me where I stood with my knees banging together. I nodded Jerry killed the ball high and to the right with this tiny little draw as it flew over the hill. We wouldn't see this ball until after Porky's next shot, but it had landed to the left of a big tree that separated the 14th and 16th fairways, about 50 yards past Pork's drive.

Porky had only one shot: a 3-wood that would put him about 125 to 130-yards from the green. He executed perfectly.

Jerry pulled his 3-wood and as he was about to swing, Porky went into his choking/spit up routine. "You OK," Jerry asked nonchalantly, not even looking over. Then he hit the most beautiful 3-wood I have ever seen, about 12 feet from the pin for an eagle, the first one I had ever seen on the Shorehaven 16th.

It was Porky's turn as he mumbled a few sarcastic remarks, loud enough for Jerry to hear as ol' Porky hit his third shot about 15 feet from the hole. Porky was away—he would putt first.

He did, and made his birdie putt.

In order for Jerry to win the hole he had to make his putt; about 12 feet from the hole.

It got really quiet. You could almost hear Porky breathe. But Jerry wasted no time, stepped right up and knocked his EAGLE into the hole.

Porky is one down. Since this is match play and the Porky Press, the lowest score on each hole is what counts. Jerry wins this one.

The Shorehaven 17th is a long 190 yards to a very narrow green. The pin was in the back with a little wind to hit though—200 to 205 yards. Now the players are getting serious.

Jerry and I hustled over to the 17th tee, about a 50 yard walk, grabbed a handful of grass and threw it up into the air to check for wind. No wind.

Jerry grabs his four iron and the ball lands on the front and rolls up to maybe 10 to 12 feet from the hole. Porky hits a beauty, but it doesn't bite and rolls to the back of the green, maybe 15 feet, for an easy par. Jerry seizes the moment and sinks yet another putt, this time for a birdie.

As we walk over to the 18th tee Jerry quietly says to me, "We're playing with his money now."

Jerry's tee shot splits the fairway leaving him a little seven to the green.

Moaning and mumbling to himself, Porky splits the fairway and lands opposite Jerry. Unable to see the green, both players guess and end up on either side of the cup with a 12-foot putt each. Being away, Porky putts and misses a makable putt. Jerry got a good read on Porky's putt and makes yet another birdie.

Let's recap. Jerry makes a 3 on 16, a 2 on 17, and a 3 on 18. Porky, despite the tricks and intimidation, had his ass handed to him on the last three. It seemed that Jerry had been coasting along for the first 16, toying with Porky. Then on the final three he decided to take charge and lay some hurt on his opponent. I suspect that four under on the last three holes at Shorehaven has never been duplicated.

Jerry smiled at Porky, gave him a little salute, and walked back to the club house as if he did this every day.

That evening the top was up on the pink Caddy as it left the parking lot. I didn't stick my thumb out for a ride—I just let it cruise on by.

I had respect. And Jerry had the cash.

CHAPTER EIGHT

Our War / Not Our War

Score High or Die

This segment relates to any summer of any year almost anywhere. Graduation! Generalities are common but true to this point. Once the senior of any class wakes up with no place to go in the morning, it hits home like a ton of bricks.

Right after graduating, back in the day, circa the late fifties to early or mid- sixties, kids were not automatically thinking of college, let alone planning to go. This was mainly because, for the most part, family members were in WWII and never had the chance to go. So, there was not a lot of "go to college" pressure being heard.

Others went off to college only to be chased around by Uncle Sam. You had to maintain good grades or be drafted right out of college. Once the draft board was running out of eligible young men, the stakes got a little higher and every male student had to take a test. It was called "Score high or die"!

Not too many years after the Viet Nam War, the draft board no longer drafted young men. Instead, the forces now work as a volunteer armed force. It was rumored that too many of the politician's kids were getting drafted so they changed the rules. Elected officials doing and accepting something the average American was not entitled to? Really?

A Whole Lifetime Ahead

Wow! Graduation Day. You spend a dozen or more years of your life working your way to this one special day; walk across the stage, get a dummy piece of paper (your actual diploma will be mailed to you), shake hands with the principal, party hard afterward, maybe lose your virginity, wake up with a hangover, and then what?

No place to go. Nothing to do. Nothing to look forward to. And a whole lifetime ahead.

This is the beginning of the great scattering. For three years you've been a unit. Buddies. Lovers. Haters. At least there was something to attach you to the others.

Now this person works hard all summer, saves their money, and in the fall goes off to college to study ecology or something. Another starts to work full time in the family

TV and appliance store knowing that the America dream included color TVs in every room. Guys like Terry join their father at the body shop, got married, build a house nearby, and like (more or less) lived happily ever after.

Some took wing for places afar. For example, the Beautiful Sisters, Cathy and Bev Snow, took Horace Greely's advice and went west to the bright lights of Las Vegas where they became 'somethings'—no one was ever quite sure what, although there were plenty of rumors. They occasionally returned to Norwalk for special events, referring to it as "the old country" and looking at us as if were rustic curiosities. After being away for a while myself, I had an idea of how they felt.

Within a year or so of graduation many of the young lovers had partaken of the sacrament of Holy Matrimony. In a few cases the shotgun was painted white making the wedding more formal. In other cases, the gestation period was foreshortened by several weeks or even months.

For every one of us males who graduated, there was the specter of Uncle Sam hovering around the front door. He was inviting us to travel to that exotic place known as Vietnam, where it rained every day, populated by people who all looked alike, except that some of them had guns and would kill you. It was in all the travel and cruise brochures.

First, the good Uncle came for the unmarried, childless, non-college men. (Now we were considered "men" whereas only a few short months ago we were just "kids.") Then the college students were on the list. The only way to escape was to maintain great grades. Then came the special tests, "Score high or die," was the rallying cry.

Between 1964 and 1973, if you were a male with a heartbeat, your chances of taking the Vietnam vacation were pretty good. A lot of these guys didn't come home. That War took over 65,000 American lives, including several of Norwalk's finest. Of those who did survive, many wished they hadn't, and never got over the trauma. And, of course, the ultimate irony, we lost the war. Or did we win? Why were we even there?

The Green Door Leads To Vietnam

Back in Norwalk, when and/or if a guy had some free time, he might cruise on down to the Calf Pasture Beach, there to find and appraise some lovelies, or discover another teen on free time in his ride and, if the gods were smiling, a six pack of coldies.

Cars of the era were behemoths compared to today and there would be a big space between the grille and the radiator. This was (according to those who should know) a custom built-in to accommodate beer. A six-pack, or even a whole case, could be stowed securely.

If stopped by the police, the driver was usually asked for license and insurance card. It was rare that the officer would ask you to step out of the car, but if they did, it was to open the trunk. (Few, if any, cars had a button on the dash that opened the trunk remotely) We never stored beer in the trunk and the police never looked behind the grille.

It's a lovely, warm, sunny late spring afternoon and we find our hero, Woody, leaning back in his black '61 Chevy convertible looking out over the sparkling Long Island Sound. Then along comes Robert in his hot rod '55 Chevy painted eyeball blue, radio blaring, screeching to a stop beside Woody.

"Hey, man. What's doing?" they both say at the same time. Of course, it comes out like "Hey man. Wat's dune?"

"I need to talk," Robert explains.

"Sure. Hop on in."

So, Robert shuts down, turns off the radio, carefully retrieves his six-pack from behind the grille, and joins Woody. They light up fresh ones and pass the church key back and forth.

"Hey," asks Woody, "is this something serious, or what?"

"No," Robert responds. "Something you only dream about just happened to me."

"OK. Let's hear it."

It was right after spring break. Robert was working at the B&T Texaco afternoons and weekends and was just hanging around until his shift started in about a half hour. The phone rang.

"Hey, can you get it?" yelled the guy on duty.

"Good afternoon, B&T Texaco. How can I help you?" Robert was very well trained and polite.

A very soft female voice announced that she had a flat tire and needed someone to change it.

"Sure," Robert assured the soft female voice. "Can you tell me where the car is, please?"

"Oh sure," she replied. "at the Stoney Run Art School."

"Handle it," the on duty guy said. "Whatever you charge you can keep for yourself."

Wow! Such a deal. Robert grabbed a fresh B&T T-shirt so he wouldn't get his dirty. The name on the shirt was 'John,' a guy who had just quit. His madras shorts stayed. "Take the wagon," the boss yelled. That was a '57 Ford wagon with tools for almost any on the road repair. And off he went.

He was, however, a couple of answers short. Like "what make of car," "what color," and "where was it parked in the lot."

The story was interrupted by Woody's request for the church key and a light.

"So, I made the rounds of the parking lot and spotted a car with a flat tire over near the boundary wall." Robert continued. "I figured that had to be it."

He unloaded his toolbox and looked around for the keys. On the seat? Behind the sunshade? In the ash tray? Nope, nope and nope. How was he supposed to get the trunk open to get the spare?

Robert shrugged and walked over to the School front

door, went inside and came face-to-face with the stern-faced receptionist.

"Can I help you?" she asked all gimlet-eyed.

Robert explained, which seemed to soften her a bit. "Yes," she responded with a sudden smile. "Go into the lobby, over to the waterfall, turn right, it's the second green door in the middle of the hall." Her finger pointed in the general direction.

Before we get to the next part, there are a few things you need to know about Robert.

He was a tall, handsome, eighteen-year-old, very polite virgin who had been taught to open doors for women and assist them in any way possible when they were in need or in distress. He had never seen a real, LIVE, actual, naked woman in the flesh.

So, when he got to the green door he rattled the knob to alert anyone inside and pushed the door open.

It was a figure drawing class and in the middle of the room, posed on a blanket on a big table was the model—completely nude. At first Robert didn't see the students. Then one of them asked, "Can we help you?"

Robert's mouth opened, but no sound came out. His knee crashed into a cast iron heat radiator by the door and the pain shot through his leg. His eyes never left the model, who turned to him with a slight smile.

"Oh, uh, yes," he stuttered, trying to focus. "I'm here to fix the flat tire. I need the, uh, trunk keys to get the spare tire..." His voice trailed off.

"Of course, silly me," the model swiveled around, dropped her long legs onto the floor and walked over to him wearing only a key ring.

Robert stopped breathing for a very long time, staring at the nude model, her breasts still bouncing in slo-mo from the walk across the floor. She looked down at the fresh gash on Robert's knee and the slow drip of blood running down his shin. "I'll be finished here soon. Wait for me at the car," she smiled brightly, walked back to her perch on the table, and resumed her pose.

Outside the room Robert resumed breathing. The receptionist called out, "Did you find the car owner?" And when Robert gave her a thumbs up she added, "How did you like her?" and laughed loudly.

He swapped out the flat for the spare, marking the nail hole with yellow chalk so that the repairman could find it more easily, and was sitting in the B&T Texaco station wagon writing up the bill, noting that the classes must be over because the parking lot was quickly emptying. The passenger door opened and there she was, wearing a short raincoat and a big smile.

"Hi." A sudden gust of wind blew the coat open and, once again, Robert was treated to the sight of a beautiful nude women who, incidentally, was at that moment climbing into his car. She took a tissue out of her coat pocket and began dabbing at the gash on his knee.

Situations and hormones often work in a cooperative fashion, as they did now. The oak tree growing in Robert's madras shorts tightened up the material and prevented her from getting full access to the wound. Without hesitation she unzipped his fly. The oak exploded out and stood at full height.

Before Robert knew what was happening, she had slipped off the raincoat, slipped her warm, wet tongue into his mouth, straddled him and slipped his oak into a place where it had never been before. Then she did her pony-express-rider-carrying-urgent-mail routine.

Robert told Woody that he saw fireworks, heard bells and whistles and car horns, and his breath came in short gasps. It was all so incredible that he managed to do it twice before she delivered the mail.

"You're incredible," she whispered in his ear. "How much is it?" she asked. "The bill for changing the flat," she added when he looked puzzled.

"Oh, uh, $15," he stammered as he furiously reviewed what had just happened.

She handed him a crumpled $20 from her coat pocket. "Johnny," she breathed looking at the name on his T-shirt, "here's $20. Next time buy some beer. I'll call you next week at the gas station. I have the number."

She gave him a quick kiss, slipped out of the car and was gone in a New York minute, leaving Robert/Johnny dazed, confused, $20 richer, and very pleased with himself.

Back in the car, both Robert/Johnny and Woody looked at their watches at the same time and realized they both had to be somewhere else and were running late. The story would have to be continued at a later date. They each left 20 feet of fresh Firestone rubber on the pavement as a memento of their hasty departure.

The warm spring turned into the hot and sunny Norwalk summer which morphed into the colorful fall. Woody and Robert ran into each other a few times, exchanged greetings and salutation, but that was all. Until one night in October, Indian summer, when Woody was having a butt-'n-a-beer in the Chevy early in the evening down at the beach. The parking lot was almost empty when, in the rear view, Woody sees Robert's Chevy come up from behind and park beside him, radio blaring. Robert shuts down, gets the six-pack, and walks around to Woody's passenger door.

"Thought I might find you here," he says with a smile. "Remember the nude model and the flat tire?"

Woody nods, opening a beer.

"Are you ready for part two?" Robert asks.

Woody nods affirmative and settles back in the seat, looking out over the Sound.

"Sure as hell," Robert begins, "she calls the B&T next week on Thursday looking for Johnny."

And on every Thursday following Johnny gets a call, takes the B&T station wagon, leaves for the afternoon, and returns all satisfied looking.

Odd thing is the names. The nude thinks Robert is Johnny. But the nude won't tell Robert her name. Every Thursday they meet in the remote corner of a parking lot, do their business in Robert/Johnny's Chevy (much cleaner and better smelling than the B&T wagon), and she drives away—nameless. Robert doesn't know what to call her, so he calls her "The Model." He knows everything intimate about this woman except her name.

Of course, she's older, much more experienced, and assumes the role of the teacher. Robert happily becomes the student. The Model teaches Robert everything she knows over the summer and, when school was starting again, suggested that, in order to learn more, he get a copy of a book called the *Kama Sutra*. Of course, we all know now that it's an ancient Indian sex manual, but we didn't know then.

Robert figured that the place to look first for a book was the Norwalk High School library where Mother Gray (profiled elsewhere in this book) reigned supreme.

Striding confidently up to the horseshoe desk (first time in the school library) Robert says, "My girlfriend wants me to read a book called the *Kama Sutra*. Don't know who wrote it, but I want to borrow it."

Mother Gray just about soiled his tailored slacks (which matched his tie and starched, long sleeve, French cuffed shirt), grabbed Robert by the arm and escorted him to the side of the room.

"Lower your voice," Mother hissed insistently. "Follow me," mincing down the aisles, finding the book, handing it to Robert, and leading him back to the desk to sign it out.

"You have it for two weeks," Mother instructed. "If you don't return it on time, you'll be assessed a penalty."

The few students looking might have noticed a wry smile pass over Mother's face as soon as Robert's back was turned and he was striding away, looking at the cover.

The book was a blockbuster. Robert told one person, who told two more and pretty soon the *Karma* was the most popular book in the NHS library. "What would a guy like Robert, whom no one had ever known to read a book, want this THIS book? Pretty soon everyone knew.

At this point Woody popped a beer, lit a cigarette, and called Robert "An educator."

They both laughed together.

While getting a higher education on Thursdays was great, it left six other days where nothing was happening. Robert was not a lazy guy who frittered away his time. He had met a nice young lady his own age while pumping gas one day. Her name was Kathy. They would fool around at the B&T, go to the Drive In, have something to eat, or watch the submarine races at the beach. They would meet somewhere, and she would jump into the Chevy for their date.

After a few dates down the road and Robert was practicing the lessons he learned from The Model and from the *Karma Sutra*. Kathy was smitten with her first real lover and told her friends how "the book" had changed her life. The book became even more popular and the Norwalk Public Library was getting requests, and not just from teenagers.

Kathy invited Robert to a special party. He was to pick

her up at her house, meet the parents, and be all spiffed up and social while doing it.

As he pulled into her driveway that evening, he thought the silver car in the driveway looked kind of familiar, but he shook it off.

Ding Dong. Kathy's father greets Robert at the door. "Nice to meetcha," and all that small talk.

As if you hadn't guessed already, Kathy's mother takes a quick look out of the bedroom window down to the driveway and immediately recognizes Robert's (sex machine) car and her heart stops immediately. She goes downstairs contemplating her worst nightmare: Her daughter has been glowing and cheerful the past few weeks. Oh my God! He's been teaching her the *Kama Sutra* plus everything I taught him.

She walked into the living room, holding herself together, where Robert and Kathy's Dad were talking cars.

'Hi Mom," Kathy burbles in delight, "this is Robert. Robert this is my Mom."

Robert was flabbergasted. Here was The Model, completely dressed, ashen, thin-lipped, wide-eyed, and terrified.

"Hello, ma'am," Robert finally gets the words out, avoiding her eyes.

"Hello Johnny—I mean Robert," The Model stammers.

Kathy thought it all very odd, but said nothing. Her father didn't even notice and said, "The fan belts on those '56's were always breaking, weren't they?"

"Have a safe time tonight," The Model called as the young couple left. Robert thought the word "safe" had a hidden meaning.

The date was a disaster.

Robert was worried sick that his past adventures, so exciting at the time, were all coming back to destroy him. He would lose The Model and Kathy. The Model's husband, whom rumor had it was mobbed up, would have him killed. As soon as the story got around parents across the area would forbid their daughters to have anything to do with him. Husbands across the area would be gunning for him. Wives, too, including a few that might be seeking more proof that Robert was a real student of the *Kama Sutra*.

After the party Robert and Kathy headed for the submarine races at the beach. Robert's submarine nose-dived to the bottom and laid there, limp and useless. Kathy wondered what had happened.

Dropping her off afterward Robert drove away so slowly that a cop pulled him over.

"What the hell is wrong with you?" the cop wanted to know. "This is a 35 and you're driving like five miles an hour in a hot car. Are you drunk?"

Robert blurted out a partial truth. "Sorry, Officer. I just broke up with my girlfriend."

"Oh," the cop's attitude changed. "I understand. Well anyway, get out of here, son. Have a few beers with your buddies, and it'll all pass soon." The cop turned away and then faced Robert again. "And drive somewhere close to, but under, the speed limit, please. Otherwise, you'll get stopped again."

The next few days were rough for our hero. Apparently, he had also been instructing other older women in the ancient Indian arts and Kathy found out. Not about her mother's involvement though, which was about the only positive element in the mess. So that was the end of that.

The Model found him and instead of riding the pony, told him that if he ever contacted her daughter again, she would ensure that her husband's New York associates would cut his dick off, somewhere close to his neck. "It's his only daughter. He's very protective," she said ominously.

"She had a wad of money. Travel money she called it," Robert told Woody. "You get it if you leave the state by the end of the week and we never see you again for a long time." She waved the money in front of his face. "Otherwise, my husband calls his friends. Capisce?"

Robert was Irish, but he understood Italian well enough, and nodded. She threw the money on the floor of his car, walked to her silver convertible, and made the rocks fly as she peeled away.

Wow! Woody thought. So, the summer love saga was ended.

Their rental limit of the beer was over and the parking lot was empty—too late in the year for swimming; too early in the evening for submarines—so they stepped behind a convenient bush and let go.

"I'm honored you picked me to hear your story," Woody

said. "Maybe I'll write it down some day."

Robert was embarrassed. "It's OK," Robert said. "I just had to tell someone cause I'll be gone tomorrow. You can tell people that I left. Probably never coming back."

"Where you going?"

"I got an uncle in Atlanta. Stay there for a week or so. Then I'm going to sign up. Help America save the world from the Gooks."

"Which branch?"

"Navy I think," Robert popped the top on the last beer and took a big slug. "I want to help, but I don't want to get too close to Mr. Charlie. I hear that a grandmother or a kid in a diaper can be a Cong and shoot your ass off" He laughed nervously. "I want to be twenty miles out at sea shooting big cannons at them."

Robert passed the open beer to Woody and he drained it.

"You know," Robert said wistfully getting out of the car. "I saw this movie with Dustin Hoffman, *The Graduate*, the other night. It almost made me throw up. No really. I had to take my date home early it upset me so much. Reminded me of The Model and Kathy and all of the others."

Robert fired up the Chevy, gave Woody a quick wave, and drove off. Nobody around Norwalk ever saw him again. Years later Woody checked for Robert's name on the Vietnam Memorial in Washington, but didn't find it.

Maybe Robert did his stint 'helping save America,' found a nice girl and eager student, settled down and used his hard-earned education for good. I certainly hope so.

Walk a Mile in My Boots

On New Year's Day 1967, I made a decision. I would up my draft and get it over with. There were a number of reasons.

First: a couple of romantic relationships had suddenly become extremely complicated and I felt that (maybe) it would be prudent if my future activities were away from Norwalk for a time.

Second: I was tired of looking over my shoulder waiting for the draft board to call my number. I had done very well at Junior college, making the Dean's list every semester. Not too many people who knew me would believe that, but it was true.

Third: I then transferred my transcript up to the university and was accepted. But I felt that I was in school for the wrong reason—just to beat the draft!

It just wasn't me, so I walked away from school, my business, my friends, and went to meet Uncle Sam in person.

Along with several other young terrified young men, I went to Grand Central station in New York. There we were joined by over a hundred more terrified kids going into the Army.

We rode over to Ft. Dix, just a few miles from Trenton, New Jersey, where we were yelled at and intimidated for hours by several drill sergeants. Not because they were trying to help us or anything, but because that's what they did for a living.

However, Ft. Dix did not have room for us (typical Army) and we boarded a plane to Ft. Benning, GA.

Many of the new inductees had never been on a plane before, so you imagine how loud it was with a hundred and thirty first time fliers on board. When I looked around, I realized I was one of the oldest, if not the oldest.

The New York guys were wild. They had brought enough booze and pot to fuel a decade of parties. The Captain announced that he was going to pass a few duffel bags around and the boys could discard unacceptable items without getting in trouble.

The officers probably had a few wild parties stocked by those duffel bags!

As well as the usual consumables, the bag would eventually contain knives, a few guns, brass knuckles, and other items of street warfare.

Ft. Benning. We're tired, sober, and cowed. And they didn't have any room for us either. It seemed that the only place on earth where Uncle Sam had room for us was in Vietnam!

Back on the plane and up to Ft. Jackson, SC. Who knew the Army has so many forts?

The usual intimidation and abuse began again when we landed in pitch darkness, were marched to an unknown location, and told to crawl under the barracks to pick up and discard any garbage we found. Of course, someone yelled "There's a rat!" Fucking great! But that turned out to be bullshit.

Then we were all treated to a fresh hair cut (Army style). No more Elvis pompadours or sideburns. Gone were all the greasy long hair guys. We were all equals. It's a lot less frightening when everyone looks the same—except for some guys who had tattoos on their shaved skulls.

That's when the magic happened. We got our Army uniforms; everything we needed from head to toe! This was done in a matter of minutes. No hesitating, eyeing up the wearer, measuring the inseam, or asking which side you dressed on.

We were all in a long line and, as we approached the dispensing area, an enlisted man eyed us quickly and yelled out the sizes to the guys handing out the uniforms!

That is the way to provide uniforms for over a hundred guys in a matter of minutes. Well! Guess who got size 14 leather boots and size 14 100% wool socks? The remainder of my uniform was a perfect fit.

Next, we were ordered to disrobe right where we stood and put on our nice, new, crisp uniforms—which we did.

Once I realized the BIG MISTAKE on the footwear, I was dumb enough to tell a very southern, skinny, little, old E9 the problem I had.

He stood about inch from my face and screamed "THE ARMY DOES NOT MAKE MISTAKES! Now get your dumb Yankee ass back in line."

I gulped, "Yes sir," and before I could tum away, I was

grabbed by the arm, spun around, and again from one inch or less I heard, "DON'T 'SIR' ME YOU ASSHOLE! I WORK FOR A LIVING!" Followed by, "So put your shit down and give me 50 push-ups!!" That was my breezy welcome to the US Army.

Lesson One Learned: Do not question the wisdom of the US Army!

We got our bunk assignments, were relieved of our civilian clothing, and marched to the four-star restaurant that actually had a view. After all it was on top of Tank Hill. One thing I learned very quickly:

Lesson Two Learned: Do not bitch about the food!

In the morning we had some eggs (they kind of looked like eggs) and grits which all of us Yankees learned to eat or else go hungry. Then we went on a five-mile walk/run to see the rest of the landscaped campus.

We did a lot of neat things that first day.

I got to do another 50 push-ups because I saluted a second lieutenant with a cigarette in my right hand. It happened right in front of the charming E9 I had been introduced to the previous night. And he remembered me.

Our daily routine was pretty much the same for the next few days.

I forgot to mention that I was also allergic to wool. That and running/marching in size 14 boots, when I usually wore a 10 narrow, caused some foot discomfort.

I was afraid to say anything because the E9 was not too fond of me. However, he did often offer a cheery "Good morning" to me, followed by crude aspersions on professional life of my mother, father (unknown), siblings and the usual including, "Did you mother have any children who lived."

By the end of second week my bunk mate saw my feet one night and reported to our nice guy Drill Sergeant. Honestly, he was a good guy.

What my bunk mate said to the DS: "His feet are such a bloody fucking mess that he better have someone look at them before something bad happens."

So, our kindly Drill Sergeant came over, took one look at my feet, gagged slightly and said, "Go up to the Captain's office. Go on sick call in the morning and have someone take a look at those feet." He seemed impressed. At least he didn't disparage my family heritage.

The following morning, I went to the Captain's office. Life pays serious tricks. The man working as Captain Davis assistant was my new best friend, the skinny, old, southern E9. He was almost nice until I told him about my feet and the DS telling me to go on sick call. He then took me outside and referred to the conversation we had a couple of weeks past about the Army not making mistakes.

I agreed that this was not caused by a mistake, but rather just something that happened outside the purview of the Army. Perhaps something that I had done on my own time to cause this problem? "Most likely," I agreed. "Yes, that's the only answer," he agreed.

He did send me on sick call and even got me a ride in a Jeep which was a blessing because the hospital was miles away.

Like all hospitals there was a Waiting Room where I waited for several hours, which was fine with me. At least I didn't have to march anywhere.

Eventually my name was called, and I was ushered into a curtained cubicle to see Captain Howard Levy.

He did not look like your typical Army officer. His shoulder bars were not polished to a high shine. His shirt was wrinkled and not the usual starchy fit.

I told my story (making the Army wrong in a few instances) and he laughed for a few seconds, before admitting me to the hospital to see if he could get the swelling down and stop the blood from weeping into my socks and boots.

I returned after three days to my unit, but with no replacement boots or socks, because I would have had to deal with my E9 buddy and his Army which did not make mistakes. Somehow, I got through several more weeks with only one other trip to the hospital

My E9 buddy kept his eyes on me whenever he could, and I did my best not to screw up. But my eyes told him a different story. And he understood and remembered.

One day our Drill Sergeant told us to get as much rest as possible because we were going to go on a forced march of several miles. That would be followed up by some nighttime maneuvers. He referred to it as a "bivouac," meaning a long march, then compulsory fun and war games, camping, and fireside chats. So, we rested when we had some free time.

We were getting close to the end of basic training. I had

concerns, but what could I do under the circumstances?

So, on the appointed day, off we go on a run-run fast march that seemed to last forever. I tried not to think of my feet in my size 14 clodhoppers. I wore multiple layers of socks, insoles and anything to try to fill up the cavernous boots. I was frightened to take them off, afraid knowing what I'd find.

Late in the afternoon we were dead on our feet, tired, quiet, hungry, and dreaming about a cold beer. Once we got our shit together— meaning a tent up, latrine dug, and a meal down—we were told to get plenty of rest because tomorrow was going to be a very tough day.

The Drill Sergeant stopped by to take a look at my feet and this time he almost threw up his dinner. The blood on the left foot had soaked through the layers of wool socks and dried and the minute I started to remove them, the bleeding started in earnest.

He took a look at the other foot and it was the same. "Report to the sick call office in the morning and tell them that I sent you."

Okay. I went to sleep thinking about how much fun that asshole E9 was going to have with me.

Bright and early I hobbled right into the sick call office and reported directly to Captain Davis. He said, "See the Master Sergeant in the other office and he'll get you a pass to the hospital. And good luck with those feet," he added sincerely.

So, I entered the lion's den and was pretty surprised

that the skinny old asshole was pretty decent toward me and wrote out the pass for me to the hospital.

He then told me to sit down and he would be right back. Little did I know that he told the soldiers outside to give me instructions on how to get to the hospital on foot—no transport!

No wonder he was being so civil toward me. I soon learned that the hospital was over 11 miles away and here I was, a recruit, a kid, a nothing to the Army, straight in from bivouac in full gear including helmet, pack, rifle and raincoat. (It was raining. Of course it was raining!)

I started walking.

Now an E1 marching alone along the side of the road in full gear in the rain in an Army fort is an unusual sight. Which drew the attention of the roaming MPs. They pushed me around a bit, yelled "What the hell are you doing?" a few times, called my E9 torturer, and drove away.

It was mid afternoon when I got to the front door of the hospital, taken to a room. I was near physical and mental collapse. The only thing holding me upright was my boiling hatred of the E9.

The nurse helped me get the boots off, cut away the blood-soaked green wool, and admitted me.

Captain Levy came in and was so pissed off when he saw my feet you would have thought I was a close relative. I also noticed that he was a little nervous—you might say jumpy.

He treated my feet with various potions and salves and

left instructions with the nurse.

A few minutes later I heard a commotion coming from his office. This whole affair was becoming a bad movie: Doctor Levy was being handcuffed and taken away by a couple of MPs. Naturally, this kind of shook me up and I feared I would be sent back to continue with the camping trip and my E9 buddy.

It was soon the talk of the ward. Captain Howard Levy, Army doctor, had been arrested for (among other things) protesting the Viet Nam war in a demonstration in town where he had been seen by the Army brass. He also, apparently, disobeyed a direct order to teach medical procedures to a Green Beret unit.

I found out later that he was found guilty of all charges and spent some 30 months in an Army stockade. He later returned to NYC and continued his medical career. Just another example of the draft capturing another victim to be sacrificed on the Vietnam altar.

I on the other hand listened to all this gossip for the next couple of days as my feet, now exposed to the light and air, took their own sweet time to heal. Quite honestly, I thought they were doing pretty well, covered in various greasy and creamy medicines.

I could stare down at them, stuck on the end of my legs like lumps of rare hamburger meat. Wiggling my toes made them look like hamburger come alive. It was eerie.

I had plenty of time to wonder what they were going to do with me. Send me back to the fun and games? They'd have to get me a new pair of boots to start with. I convinced a pretty nurse to drop the bloody 14s, along with the ruined green woolies, into the trash. Now I was barefoot, and even the US Army wouldn't approve of that.

Early one morning a nurse came in to tell me a replacement doctor had been assigned to replace Doctor Levy, and would be in to see me today. Well good news/bad news, never knowing the next step always breeds stress, no matter how old you are. So, it was sit and wait quietly—which I did.

The replacement doctor looked and muttered several unsavory things about my feet, the Army, and the condition of the world in general.

"I'm going to discharge you from the hospital," he announced. My heart sank. I saw more horrible E9s and rice paddies in my future before a violent demise. "I'm also going to request that you be discharged from the Army," he continued. "You can fight that if you want. You're unfit for service." He looked at me seriously. I stared back, keeping my mouth shut and trying not to look too disappointed.

I must have had the fastest and smoothest discharge in Army history. After a quick visit to the Captain (wearing my comfy size 10 narrow civilian shoes) who wished me good luck, and a stop so the E9 could issue travel orders and a plane ticket, I was back in Norwalk with a smile on my face. The old place never looked any better.

Some time later I realized that the Army's hurry-up-and-leave routine had a purpose. If I had stayed in thrall

to Uncle Sam for a single day longer, I would have been
eligible for military benefits and a pension.

My favorite Uncle is also a penny-pinching bastard.

CHAPTER NINE

The Doyles Of Norwalk

I lived in our house at the center of the universe for 18 years. There was Curly (Dad), Ellie (Mom), John (my older brother), me and, eventually the Red-Haired Screamer, Colleen (my sister).

When you're a kid, growing up somewhere, you get the impression that your place, your home, your house, is at the center and everything else—neighborhood, earth, sun, universe—revolves around it. I know I was like that growing up in Norwalk, CT.

Around my house the neighborhood was a bit like the United Nations.

The Doyle family was Irish—right to the tips of our shamrocks and the Irish Whiskey that tickled (or pickled) our livers.

The family to the right were Polish. The husband was a great guy who gave my brother a car—a '40 Pontiac coupe,

I think. The wife, on the other hand, couldn't speak a word of English and was determined to find and keep any of my golf balls which might accidently end up in her garden.

On the left were the Rizzos. Tony, the dad, only came home on the weekends. The rest of the time he stayed at his apartment in New York. As far as I recall, the family— Grace and the boys, Ralph and Tony, Jr—never visited him. Tony wore black, was polite and was the boss.

Grace (she was the one who set up the fabulous food tent after the Shorehaven Golf Club fire and kept me fed all summer) was wonderful. She was an Italian War bride who mangled English, taught everyone how to play cards, gamble, make pizza and swear in the most eloquent Italian.

She was more American than most Americans. Between Grace and the two boys, their '57 Chevy had every piece of sheet metal replaced at least once.

Behind the Rizzos were the LeCounts. They were from France, spoke English with a pursed French accent, and were incredibly pretentious. Saying a neighborly "Hello" or waving "Good morning" got nothing in return. We referred to them as "The Frogs."

Next door to The Frogs lived the Klines, two dear, sweet people from Germany. Mrs. Kline had lost much of her hearing from Allied bombings. Their son, Leo, visited a few times. A former German World War II soldier, he was much older. He would show us where an American GI bullet was still lodged in his back. You could see the entry scar in the front, but no exit would in the back.

Across the street was brother John's Garden of Eden with five girls—all ages and configurations—a vamp of a mother and a happy husband who had his own bedroom and his own sense of freedom.

Albert worked two or three jobs, was loved by everyone (except, possibly, his wife), and was always there to lend a hand in an emergency or when a neighbor was working on a project.

Not to be unfair with my assessment of the mother, Albert smoked those awful little, black cigars and, did I mention, drank—a lot! He was also fearless. Once, at a neighborhood party, Frank was flying high when someone bet him $20 he would not eat a sandworm sandwich.

Sandworms, also known as lugworms, are really ugly critters, six to eight inches long who live in the tidal sand, and are used as bait for striped bass and flounder. They are sold in bait shops in the northeast.

That makes them really gross (in addition to looking big, wet, reddish, and really gross) is their mouth—a sort of sucker with teeth. I once picked one up when fishing, it grabbed my arm with its mouth, and the next thing I'm bleeding.

Anyway, Frank can't resist the dare, weaves off to the local bait shop down by the Sound, and comes back in 45 minutes grinning with his sandworms in a plastic bag.

In front of the entire party, he plops the wriggling worms onto the hot grill ("You didn't think I was gonna eat 'em raw?" he exclaims in mock dismay.) until they're still and brownish, puts a couple between a hamburger bun, adds some lettuce and mayo, and downs it. And collects $20. To this day I shudder and get goose bumps just thinking about it!

Then there was Rusty, our resident little person.

One morning Mom was in the kitchen getting breakfast ready when she screamed so loud everyone immediately came running. She explained that she had seen a little person turn over a garbage can, get inside, and roll down the driveway to the street.

Since this was about 7:00 am we knew that Mom's two-beers-a-day habit had not set in yet, so we all manned a window to see what would happen next. Sure enough, this miniature kid comes up his driveway, pulls another garbage can, gets inside, and rolls noisily down the driveway.

Rusty also had an older, normal size, shapely sister, Marylou. We all (John, me, Marylou, and Rusty) all became great friends and classmates until John got his driver's license, after which there apparently was never any room in the car for Rusty or me.

Up on the back street we had family. Mom's brother, uncle Jim, arrived home fresh from WW II with a German bride and his War pay. He bought an old car from my Dad (something like a '35 Plymouth) and drove his bride across her new country and back before settling down near us.

They soon had company who stayed forever, literally. The bride's mother and a guy named Ziggy moved in. Ziggy was a mystery man; apparently unrelated. Except for

Uncle Jim, everyone spoke German and they all got along famously. Uncle Jim and the bride had five kids and they all looked like their mother and father. So, we were never sure where Ziggy fit in.

Further up the street were the Hyman family with daughters Carol and Claudia—who was my first girlfriend. Always one to impress the girls, I once ate a raw potato on a bet. I was sick for the next day and, to this day, there had better not be any lumps in my mashed potato.

I don't remember the circumstances, but in the space of one afternoon John punched Carol in the nose and made the blood flow while their dog bit me in the ass. Mom had to deal with Mr. Hyman as well as the emergency room where I got a shot and stitches.

We all went to somewhere between five and seven schools—including Norwalk High School for the last three years. My first was Jefferson and Uncle Louie warned me that if I went into the classroom, something terrible would happen to me. So, I refused to go in and sat stubbornly on a chair outside the door. Dad's foot in my backside convinced me that the teacher would never do that inside the room, so I joined the class.

Sometimes when John was in the same school we'd walk home together. Mom would meet us halfway with fudge—a real treat with or without nuts.

One day on our way home near the school we ran into a girl standing at the edge of a school wall by a ditch, maybe 20 feet deep.

"I'm going to jump," she said. Then she said it a few more times. "I'm going to jump."

I guess John got tired of her empty threats and gave her a little push. The screams could be heard all over South Norwalk. There was a thud when she landed in some soft sand, but she was OK.

The teachers didn't see the humor in the situation and dragged John off to the principal's off with me in tow. Sitting outside the office I could hear John crying as they made him promise that he would never do anything like that again.

Then we had to wait for Mom to show up—no fudge on this trip—and she gave John a few shots on the back of the head because she was angry. Then, of course there was the "Wait 'til your father gets home!" to deal with.

When that happened John got a bright red butt and once again made to promise that he'd never do anything like that again.

To the best of my knowledge, John never pushed anyone off a cliff again, though I'm sure the urge must have crossed his mind at one time or another.

Cue The Irish Tenor

Dad had a high, Irish, tenor voice and there were three times a year when we got to hear it at its finest.

One such occasion was at Christmas.

I recall the Christmas Eve that Dad came home cheeks all red and rosy like you-know-who and presented Mom with a fresh turkey for tomorrow's feast. Mom took a look at it and burst into tears. Wow! I thought. This is some turkey!

My brother, who was at that time much wiser than I, explained that at the A&P (Mom's preferred place to purchase a turkey) they did not come with full plumage. Or feet. Or a head.

Dad was so pleased with himself that he had a few more beers and sang up every Irish song known including all of the Christmas ones. It was like having Bing Crosby himself in the house.

When John and I were sent to bed on Christmas Eve, we always set out cookies and a fresh, cold Schaefer for Santa. Did I tell you? The Santa who came to our house was lactose intolerant.

Brother John was born just a few hours shy of the birthday of Ireland's patron saint, St. Patrick. Some people wanted to call him Patrick, but cooler heads prevailed. Mom always shouldered the blame and responsibility for the poor timing.

So, the days around John/Patrick's birthday brought out the Irish tenor. If the birthday was on a weekend, the songfest would last for an extra day. The only break we got was when we went to church and an old guy in bright robes would speak and chant in a foreign language accompanied by much jumping up, kneeling and sitting down.

When it came to the part about wanting money, he always spoke in English. The words varied but the subject was always about wanting more.

Mom made corned beef and cabbage for the big lunch because that's what St. Patrick would have wanted. Our little one-bathroom house always seemed smaller that day. Dad tried putting in an exhaust but somehow got intercepted after cutting the hole and before actually installing the fan. So, what we had was a rectangular hole in the wall covered with a yellow towel.

During the summer, when every relative from near and far descended on our house for the Fourth of July Picnic, the "Tears of Irish Laughter" would once again ring through the summer air. The relatives could not get enough of Dad and, to tell the truth, he didn't need much encouragement.

There were random occasions, like weddings, when Dad had reached his quota of beer and would be introduced to the wedding party. They had a choice: a Bing Crosby special or "When Irish Eyes are Smiling." What a choice!

It's A Girl!

John and I were eight and ten, and visiting one of the neighbors, when we heard the words that would forever change our lives.

"It's a girl!"

Dad was standing on the top step of our house looking like he was about to burst into the biggest and greatest Irish song ever.

A few days later Mom, Dad, and this screaming red-haired bundle of joy arrived home.

"Quiet!" It was a word we heard a lot. Quiet so Mom could get some much-needed rest. Quiet so the red-haired screamer could sleep. I mean, all she did was sleep for a few hours, wake up, smile, be bathed, have some milk, and scream for an hour before she went off to sleep again.

The biggest party in the universe, with our house as the focal point, took place to celebrate the christening of Colleen Ann Doyle. Inlaws and outlaws, friends, neighbors, beggers from downtown corners, were all invited. Even the priest had a few beers. People brought gifts and it wasn't even Christmas. Food from every nation was served and eaten with gusto. Our house, yard, driveway and garage were shoulder to shoulder. They spilled over onto the neighbors' yards.

John and I, since we were on one of the far outer rings in terms of attention decided we'd paint our bikes. Dad was doing every song known to man so long as that man was Irish. Uncle Louie, who was always a Class A shit disturber, suggested that since the bikes looked so great, we should paint each other. When that was finished, Uncle Louie took a Polaroid of us with our bikes and then announced that he was needed elsewhere immediately.

Dad was rendering his version of an Irish classic as Mom walked Aunt Kaye to her car and spotted us. She screamed once and then started to howl, long and hard and loud. Dad interrupted his song, ran around the corner, grabbed us both by our painted necks and placed a size 12 shoe in our butts several times. The party began to wind down.

Our paint, back in those pre-scientific times, was not water-based latex. It was oil based, requiring turpentine to thin it. So, John and I got a complete bath in turpentine. We ended up red and blotchy with small patches of color and smelled like a pine forest for days.

To this day I can positively say that I have (1) never bought or used turpentine, (2) have never painted anyone else, and (2) have never had anyone else paint me.

Changes Everywhere

After the arrival of Colleen, the Red-Headed Wonder, things changed around the house. Her small voice was the one Dad wanted to hear. John caught on almost immediately and remained so quiet around home that you almost had to poke him with a sharp stick to get a response. I was not a quick learner like him. Too often I had to eat a second bowl of soap suds with noodles to John's one.

John and I were the unappointed and unofficial protectors of our little sister in all things.

One day she accidently lost a tooth while playing across the street. Dad was not there and Mom didn't drive anyway, so what to do? Tooth, ice, screaming for several hours until Dad got home. John and I were not so gently reminded to pay closer attention to the welfare of our little sister so as to prevent further reddening of our butts.

Then we lost John.

He was still there in body, but his spirit had moved on. It started the night Elvis Presley appeared on the Ed Sullivan Show. Everyone was impressed. Even Dad.

The Doyle family shopped at Altman's Clothing Store and John, knowing he could put items on the family account, decided to upgrade his wardrobe. I'm at the Moore's house,, where we played after school, when John shows up in blue suede shoes, black pants with a pink stripe and matching pink shirt. He tapped his foot to the music.

Everyone thought he was so cool. Except Dad and me. Suddenly John didn't want to go with me to catch frogs. His only interests were Elvis and girls. He even wanted to dance with the girls.

Mom had sudden business in another part of the house when Dad arrived home. He looked at John, up and down, walked around him, and then exploded. Not only was he pissed that John had the audacity to go shopping on his account, he was also pissed at John's choices.

The clothes had been sized and worn so no taking back. Well, Dad decided, they were never to be worn. I was never to buy anything again without approval. The Altman's account was closed. John's days as an Elvis impersonator were over.

Of Course, We Had Cars!

Up until late 1955 we had cars, but they were old, used cars. Family sedans with small engines and great for hauling your family, groceries, and building supplies around.

Late in 1955 Dad got his first new car: a 4-door, V-8 with three-on-the-tree. Cool and a lot more power than the old flathead Fords Dad was used to. He liked to drag race just a little off the traffic lights on the Boston Post Road. I had an already cool brother (the Elvis outfit made an occasional appearance when Dad wasn't around), Dad was cool with his new car, so that made me kind of cool by just being in their shadow. So I thought. But shit happens.

We were at a gas station one Sunday, Colleen, John and I, and Dad said to turn on the key to read the gauge. I reached over the seat, grabbed the key, and turned it. Too far! I panicked and held it in the "Start" position. The car leaped forward like a horse that had just been kicked in the balls. Since it was in gear, it also wanted to keep going as my frozen hand held the key against the starter. I let go. Finally. Before the hose was ripped out of the pump and we were all engulfed in flames and died.

Anyway, it was the end of another perfect day and Dad's Irish tenor floated over yet another Norwalk neighborhood.

A couple of years later Dad bought a new '57 Chevy 2-door sedan Belair, 283 V-8, power glide, white over black. It was, very conveniently, when John turned 16, got his license, and got the car for weekend dates. Pretty soon there were fuzzy dice hanging from the rearview mirror, shirts, and dual fender mirrors.

We became a team. John at the wheel, friend Phil Orrico, Dad grudgingly enjoying the "coolness" of being in a hot car, and me (as usual) traveling in the shadows of greatness.

Of course, burning off from every light and having to be first in every line of cars on the highway took its toll on the Chevy. Dad was on his way home from work one night and the 283 expired. A blown piston. Right after he arrived home, he discovered that the car was just past the 12/12 warranty. Not looking good. The Chevy dealer said he had a great deal on a new car and, No, he was not willing to extend the warranty. Colleen never got in trouble anyway. I got a ringside seat since this was not my movie. Brother John got his ears pinned back.

The next few weeks were awkward for everyone.

Dad had to hitch a ride with friends, take the bus, or

hitch hike to the Schaefer plant in Fairfield.

John was doing postgrad work at Wright Tech in Stamford, so he towed the car there to get it out of sight and, hopefully, to fix it. The block was cracked, so he was down one engine. Somehow, he came up with a couple of hundred dollars and an engine. He needed a few weeks.

Colleen and I couldn't wait. Dinners were ugly silent affairs except when Dad decided to once again share the reasons why he had to take the bus to work. Mom would agree and offer her stories of loving the walk to the A&P which helped her keep her trim figure. Colleen might fuel the fire by commenting on how she missed the Saturday family ritual of going out in the car for ice cream. I just kept quiet.

True to his word, about three weeks later John arrived back in our driveway with the Chevy. It looked the same, but there was something about the sound that was sharply different. John had installed glasspack mufflers which, between the stone walls of the driveway, sounded loud, but cool.

Mom had a beer waiting for Dad, and one waiting for him on his arrival. The car had even been detailed.

Dad walked around the car a couple of times, smiling and nodding. Then he popped the hood. I noticed that John had backed up a few feet as if to give himself a head start if a quick escape was needed. Dad looked and muttered a few things that are not usually muttered around children.

He noticed that the valve covers were different. The

radiator seemed to have been moved forward as if to accommodate a larger engine. The exhaust manifold was closer to the steering column.

John causally explained that the upgrade to a '58 348 cubic inch engine was the right thing to do. The cost was within the budget and the addition of the 4-barrel carb was necessary, Of course the engine needed to breathe, so that would explain the dual exhaust.

Dad backed the car out of the driveway as we watched carefully. He drove away alone and although we couldn't see him, we could hear the roar of the 4-barrel and the pure scream of new glasspacks as Dad passed through maybe 50 to 60.

When he got home he walked directly past John without comment, opened a cold Schaefer, and sat down in front of the TV. John smiled a little smile. Colleen asked when she could go out for a ride.

"Tomorrow night," Dad answered. "You and I will take Mom out for ice cream."

It was many months later before Dad let John borrow the '57 for a date.

The modified '57 stayed with us for the next seven years and remained a threat on the Boston Post Road and Route 95. Once John and I got our own hot rods the '57 became a "family car." Dad and Mom and Colleen took it out on ice cream runs. Dad took it to work. It was kind of crazy to hear this cool sounding car coming around a corner and then realize it was your parents and little sister.

Dad would goose the engine as he went by just to show off.

The only damage to the '57 happened one night when a stone walls in the driveway jumped out and bit the front fender. Dad was so mad, but he never fixed or replaced the fender. He left it scratched as a reminder. Never trust a stone wall.

About this time the Chevy dealer, Old Mr. No Warranty Extension, called and said he had just the car for Dad: a '64 Chevy Impala, V-8 standard shift, 327 engine, dual exhaust, all white with a black interior. Dad smiled a funny smile and went over to the dealer who did a trade-in test ride with the '57 and had the mechanics look it over.

They made the deal of the century—wrecked fender and all. Dad was smiling again when they signed the paperwork and shook hands.

This is only the beginning of the story. Read on!

Right around this time Big Bill Kish was about to get married to the equally tall, beautiful Judy Murdoch. We called Bill "Bigfoot," only when he was out of earshot, and most Sunday mornings you could find Big Bill and several friends enjoying devotions with Dad in the driveway or in the garage.

On this particular Sunday morning Dad offered Big Bill a wedding present: the 348 engine out of the '57 Chevy. All Bill had to do was replace the 348 with a tired old 265 from a '55.

When I found about the deal with Big Bill, I questioned the purchase of the Impala.

"The deal's still on," he replied with a smile.

It took Big Bill a couple of days to make the switch and that was when the dealer called to confirm a pick up date for the Impala. Dad was a bit vague and called the dealer back after checking the newspaper. Wednesday evening was the reply.

Come Wednesday evening it was raining cats and dogs. "Why not pick up the car tomorrow? The rain is supposed to clear up."

"It's a perfect night," he replied with a smile.

The salesman didn't venture into the driving rain to reinspect the '57. "What about the new car warranty?" Dad asked. Which I thought was strange because he'd already signed everything.

"Don't worry," the salesman said. "It's perfect and it's yours."

Dad took the '64 keys, gave the salesman the '57 keys and smiled, "She's all yours." He handed the salesman the keys to the '57.

All the way home Dad smiled. The next day the Chevy dealer called about 20 times.

"What can I do," I asked. "Have your father call me," was the answer.

I knew that was never going to happen.

Finally, the dealer reaches Dad who talks, is quite firm and smiling the entire time. The end of the conversation went something like, "Hey, the '57 is the car you inspected and drove. And, by the way, my new Impala is just great.

Thanks for such a good deal and don't be bothering me again with any more phone calls."

Dad smiled every time he got into that Impala. And for all I know Bigfoot's car with the Chevy 348 might still be running somewhere back in Norwalk.

A Severe Case Of Road Rash

There are times when the usually friendly road just rears up and bites you big time. That happened to me one fateful day when I was at the B&T.

Paul Fusco and I each bought half of a motorbike, which we shared. One day around midday Paul wheeled into the B&T and said, "I have to work, so why don't you take the rest of the day off?"

It was a nice, warm early summer day so I called up Sharon, my girlfriend, and asked her if she wanted to go for a ride. "Of course!"

I was just leaving when brother John comes out with a new, white Bell helmet in his hand. "Wear this," he ordered. I had never worn a helmet before, but I put it on and felt the strange and uncomfortableness as I rode.

After a matinee by the lake with Sharon I dropped her off and headed back to the B&T. About a mile from her place, I suddenly saw something out of the corner of my eye that told me to lay the bike down.

Laying down a bike is not something you do casually. It

means consciously and suddenly leaning the bike over until it (and you) are sliding along the highway at a high rate of speed leaving quantities of metal and flesh embedded in the asphalt.

I've read that in a trauma situation where you immediately become unconscious, the brain does not have time to "remember" the details. I don't remember anything like pain, noise, crashing sounds, brakes, police sirens, people yelling, or leaving the side of my face on the road.

The next thing I remember is being in an ambulance passing the B&T and waving at Norman Wilmont who was home from the Navy. I thought there must be something wrong with him from the way he looked.

In the Emergency Room they cut off my clothes and pushed, pulled, pricked and prodded. A priest came by and gave me last rites, which really got my attention, because I was certainly not ready to die yet. Then came all of the stuff I'd been missing: pain, suffering, agony, burning, and lots of other nasty feelings.

I spent the next 25 days in hospital. I walked the last five. I was the color and texture of hamburger from head to toe. One side of my face looked quite different from what I remembered, probably from leaving the good looking part on the pavement. My nose was broken. They discovered that the day I was released.

Sharing

In 1959 my brother, John, and I together bought a nice, little '55 Studebaker, 2-door sedan, V-8 standard from our Uncle Louie for $500. (You remember Uncle Louie, the Shit Disturber.) Since John was the only licensed driver at the time, he got to call the shots. So, the car was painted green at Steve's Body Shop. They also removed some of the chrome and personalized it.

But my brother had a roving eye for cars and soon spotted a 1940 Ford coupe in Westport and bought it for something like $50. Of course, it didn't run—hence the cheap price.

No problem! John, assisted by Joe Azery, decided to tow it back to Norwalk—which was not that far in miles, but proved to be long in time.

They were charged with, among other broken laws, illegal towing, towing an unregistered car, towing a car with no lights, towing a car with no insurance, and towing a car with no seat for the driver; John was sitting like a king on an old toilet steering away.

Even though the judge was sympathetic, noting that they were being careful by towing late at night, with another car following at a proper distance so as to ward off a possible rear-ender. But he had to suspend their licenses for a year. Bang!

I could hardly hold back my tears of sorrow!

I had a freshly minted driver's license, a freshly painted Studebaker, and a brother who needed transportation to work and so on. I even had the balls to charge John for gas money. It was not his finest year.

This was also about the time we discovered Dover Drag Strip about 90 minutes away. We loaded up a couple of cars full of guys and went to watch. "We can do this," we thought.

We tuned up the Studebaker and, since Paul had just turned 18, he drove through New York in case a cop saw us. At the track we passed inspection and got ready for the practice runs with me behind the wheel.

I was a nervous wreck, but I managed to get down the strip, loving every second of it. I got to the semi-finals that first outing. Then, after a few more weeks of practice, I won four weeks in a row.

Poor John. He really missed having a car to actually drive—he could work on the Ford, but someone else had to test drive it.

He did have the girlfriend thing perfected, dating sisters Gail and Sandi at the same time/different days. The girls were both over 18 and had read *The Book* referred to in other parts of this scribble. I never discovered the details of just how they shared John.

One time I asked Gail out and she said, "No thanks, our Dad lets us use his car." Not completely sure what that meant. But I hadn't yet read *The Book*, and wasn't familiar with a *manage a trois* scenario.

Target Practice

BB guns were part of the era and every Christmas we all got the ads from the Daisy Air Rifle Company about the latest Red Ryder rifle that was just like the one Red used to subdue the bad guys or take out that pesky grizzly bear in the comic books. They even had a scheme where you could leave little printed cards on your father's chair, in his tobacco, or on his work bench announcing your gift of choice.

Naturally, having a BB gun, you wanted to shoot at something. Break something. Streetlights were a good first choice. We went with Charlie who had a good BB gun and a custom Chevy. Pump. Aim. Fire. Drive like hell. Repeat.

How about something even more exciting? Well, let's shoot out the lights over the entrance to the Silvermine Tavern while people were inside eating and drinking. That made good sense.

If BB guns were fun, a .22 rifle would be even more fun. So reasoned a bunch of guys. Fortunately, I was off caddying at Shorehaven Golf Club that day, but I was involved in their take down.

It all started when I got home from caddying. One of the local kids told me what was happening. Some of the guys had decided to go snake hunting with someone's father's .22.

I reported to Dad and in seconds we were flying down

the road. I had never seen Dad show real fear, but he was scared now. We saw some bikes pulled into the bushes at the side of the road and stopped. Soon we heard a shot and screaming. We ran into the woods and there was Junior lying on the ground holding his ankle and foot and bleeding all over the place.

Dad yelled at the nonwounded to "Get the Hell out of here." A couple of us grabbed Junior and the rifle, got him into the car, and Dad sped off toward the hospital. We had a death grip on Junior's ankle trying to (a) prevent him from bleeding to death, and (b) trying to prevent a bloody mess in the car.

Meanwhile Dad's yelling at anyone who will listen. "Who got the rifle. Who's rifle is it? Who shot Junior? Whose idea was it?"

"Bill Thayer," was the answer to all of the questions.

At the hospital Dad called Junior's parents to alert them and reassure them that Junior was not going to die just yet, but he would be on crutches for a while.

Then it was off to the Thayer house with the rifle. Mr. Thayer was a fireman and not home, but Bill's nervous and trembling mother grabbed the weapon, ran with it somewhere, and came back and began wailing on her son, angry and fearful.

Everyone with hearing in the neighborhood knew when Bill's father got home a little later.

The story, as it eventually came out, was that the four guys decided to go snake hunting in the woods with Bill's father's .22. They see a snake and Junior, thinking he would slow down the creature, tries to step on it just as Bill gets off a very accurate shot. The bullet catches Junior in the ankle, careens off the bone, and goes through two or his toes. A three for one shot!

The police were probably involved. You can't just turn up at the Emergency Room with a gunshot wound without causing some additional paperwork. But, I don't recall anyone being charged.

Bill, of course, had problems sitting for several days and the rifle and bullets were securely locked away forever. Junior hobbled about on crutches for a couple of months until everything healed up again.

As for me, it put me right off guns of all kinds. To this day the only guns I've handled are the ones Uncle Sam owned. He let me fire them once in a while under very controlled circumstances.

Learning The Big Life Lesson

John Doyle, my much older and so much wiser brother, woke up one sunny morning and decided to prolong his education. He chose to attend Wright Technical School in nearby Stamford.

I don't know what deal he made with our father about paying, but John had to continue working part time at the A&P in Darien. He would wake up in Norwalk, drive to Stamford for six hours of classes, then head back toward Norwalk and stop at the A&P just off Route 95 in Darien.

He would restock shelves, round up grocery carts in the parking lot in the rain and snow. But being the clever brother, John took a look around and thought he would be better off learning how to use a cash register. He would welcome the opportunity to stay inside and work with the young women who needed some help, or just plain needed a break, or to go home and make dinner.

Brother John would then complete the trip by returning home to Norwalk.

Going to school for something you loved, had first-hand knowledge of, and a working experience with, made it a lot easier. There still were many challenges over the two years, but John flourished and it was never "boring old school"—it was a dynamic place to be.

The following spring he retired from the A&P and started buying and working on unfinished hot rods.

Several of us realized he knew so much more than us, but we did learn by trial and error from the Master. Since late afternoon spring days were not totally uncomfortable outside, we moved ahead quickly and soon a dead hot rod came alive under the John's hands. Then he became a master salesman, and a handsome profit was made.

John also became an expert in the tedious and detailed work involved in converting hotrods from 6-volt to 12-volt wiring. Soon the V-8 engines began to roar in the old rods.

So that was his start with being able to fix cars when others gave up on them. He got married shortly thereafter and opened a Texaco gas station far from the B&T. But my Texaco was in a better location and John eventually closed down his place and moved to B&T and joined our crew of young, enthusiastic, good-looking guys who were just waiting to help motorists in any way we could.

If you look up "honest" in the dictionary, you'll see John's picture. He gave customers what they wanted, nothing more, and never over charged. We would, of course let them know if they needed new brakes, spark plugs or even a fan belt. So, it paid off being honest. Just as God would have liked, and we took it as a critical life lesson that was not always typical of the service station mentality.

So, my older brother joined forces with the B&T Beer in the Wall gang. A year or so into business, and being moderately successful, brother John sat down one day and said, "Lets go racing."

Wow! We were all excited. I mean Paul, Larry, me—

even our Dad and a few of our girlfriends.

Next John did his homework and produced a build sheet and gave us our orders: "Let's all start looking for an old Willys or a Ford from 1935 on," since that was the first year the Fords came with hydraulic brakes.

We toured our favorite junk yards in search low mileage Chevy V-8 engine with 327 cubic inches. The car, a '37 Ford 2-door coupe, was in excellent shape for its age.

Then the work began, crammed in between fill-ups, service on customer's cars, late nights and early mornings. We tore down the engine and sent it out for some machine work to make it a little bigger on the inside and prepare the bore, the heads, camshaft, and timing chain, until the entire engine was basically new again—almost a virgin.

It lay there patiently waiting for the special Hot-Rod-Go-Very-Fast parts to arrive. As you know from reading this book, we happily raced, rebuilt, retooled, and revised continually for several years; until John got his "GREETINGS" letter.

That really spelled the end of the B&T Texaco. It was so much more than just a gas station; it was part of a whole gang of young men and women who invested a part of their carefree young lives in it. We were doing what made us relish life—the sales of gas and service just paid for our enjoyment.

If Viet Nam hadn't come along, I suspect it probably would have been something else just as momentous that ended the glorious days of the B&T Texaco.

We were too young, I suppose, thinking that change would not come and destroy our world. Our little world was B&T. Not unlike the Garden of Eden where, if you did what you were told to do, all would be safe and remain the same. Carly Simon said it best when she sang out to the world that "I know nothing stays the same..."

Many of us in Norwalk grew up in the Catholic Church, went to Mass with our parents, studied the Catholic Catechism, and received our first Holy Communion—which basically confirmed us as life-long dues paying members.

And having such a good time, we discovered, was wrong. Misguided. Errant. Against the natural grain of things.

We learned from the priests—and were constantly reminded by the teaching staff of nuns—that no one on earth deserves to be this happy for very long. Adam and Eve were fine examples, and look what happened to them.

Of course, our leaders were correct. We were having way too much fun for it to continue. So, it was over for us. Just like when that letter from Uncle Sam with the word "GREETINGS" arrived. One by one we were expelled from most of what was good and loved and we soon learned, to our horror, that nothing would ever be the same again.

We can, however, pass on the good feeling. Walk around some beautiful, classic cars with your children or grandchildren. You will be telling them stories long into the night about a car you drove and the adventures you had. Many things have changed over the years, but man's love of building and driving his own personal "hotrod" has, thankfully, continued.

Memories and pride will keep it alive...

Baseball, hot dogs, apple pie, and Chevrolet,

Dinah was touring the U.S.A.,

Mickey was magic, and Willie had it in the basket,

Ryan was running, the King was crowned,

and the Shoe had it in stride,

Arnie was ready to go...

... in these simple times of the past.

The clean lines and the graceful stance of the Classic Chevrolets remain a constant reminder of those great times. A time when you could open the hood of your pride and joy and understand everything that you saw. Life and times were simple then and the '55-'56-'57 Chevys continue to be a reminder of those "wonder years." Déjà vu every time we see a Classic Chevrolet. Memories and pride will keep it alive.

— **Brian Doyle**

Acknowledgments

The people I have to thank for helping with this book are the dear people I learned the most from in the shortest amount of time. My mother and father showed the way.

My mother was the silent type and did not have any malice toward anyone, ever. I found that to be a wonderful trait. One of her favorite phrases was, "If everyone ate bologna sandwiches it would be a boring world."

Quite true! And she led me to believe we all have a choice. So, I decided to leave my own footprints in the sand and tried not to follow the herd.

My father spent Saturday shopping and sharing the chores. He would sometimes cook up some interesting meals. Then an afternoon nap was in order.

Sundays were serious, church was a ritual and listening to a priest speak Latin had to be avoided. Caddying was the answer to that.

Ralph, Hook, and Slice taught us all we needed to know: respect for others no matter how bad they were at golf, because any one of them might play a pivotal part in your future. They gave us freedom to create our own personality—to develop an interest in your "boss of the day," and to respect the ones who played silently.

Most of all they taught us to always do the best job possible, and never visit greed or envy.

Brian Doyle

About the Authors

The life of Brian Doyle, at least the first 20 or so years, is described in detail this book. Following the B&T Texaco and his short but memorable stint with the U.S. Army, Brian eventually made a life career in the golf business representing clothing and equipment makers in the Eastern U.S.

Brian is now retired and lives in Central Florida in a golf community with his wife, Sue, his rescue dog, and his restored black '57 Chevy—which he lovingly polishes and takes out in good weather.

John W Prince is a retired writer, graphic designer, and photographer who also came of age on the 1950s and '60s. He lives in Central Florida.

Made in the USA
Columbia, SC
13 September 2021